Enjoy Jesus!

Love.

R H

Col 3:17

Britt Merrick is the best "young" Bible expositor I have ever heard. *Big God* is his breakout work. With remarkable content, a fabulous presentation and the Spirit's anointing, Britt writes with the same power with which he speaks.

Jay Carty
Author and Former Basketball Player (Los Angeles Lakers)

I thank God for men who not only teach the Word accurately but also live it out. This book describes the faith God wants us to have, and Britt's life exemplifies it.

Francis Chan
Author of *Crazy Love*
Pastor of Cornerstone Church, Simi Valley, California

Britt Merrick has written a powerful, challenging, practical, exciting, and thoroughly Bible-based book that will stir your heart and convince you more strongly than ever that God is worthy of all our trust.

Wayne Grudem
Research Professor of Theology and Biblical Studies
Phoenix Seminary, Phoenix, Arizona

Pastor Britt's powerful book is well known to my family. The instruction, lessons and Spirit-filled knowledge were the basis of our Bible study for more than a year at Reality Carpinteria, where my family and I attend. *Big God* will allow those seeking a closer walk with Jesus Christ to realize the endless love that our Lord offers us every moment . . . and why our greatest goal is to live in harmony with Him. Pastor Britt's courage in the face of adversity demonstrates that he lives his life according to Scripture. Learn from this brave, humble man of God. Your family will be blessed by his great wisdom and gifts.

Kathy Ireland
Author, Entrepreneur and Model

Britt and the entire Merrick family are an inspiration to many believers, including myself. The honesty and vulnerability they witness in this book remind me of how big our God is, and it encourages me to go toward the impossible by faith.

Bryan Jennings
Professional Surfer and President of Walking on Water Ministries

The greatest defense of faith is not all of the evidence or the rationale. The greatest defense is truth backed up by a lifestyle. Britt Merrick shows us how the heroes of faith did it, how he seeks to do it and how we can too. When we embrace a big God, we will have a big faith.

Josh D. McDowell
Speaker and Author of *Evidence that Demands a Verdict* and *Evidence for the Resurrection*

I am very encouraged when I meet young leaders such as Britt Merrick. He is a voice of the future; a leader we all can follow. Not only can he tell a story and motivate a crowd, but he is also biblically solid. It doesn't get any better than this.

John M. Perkins
Author of *Follow Me to Freedom* and *Let Justice Roll Down*

God has not promised that our skies would always be blue or that the road would always be smooth. He has promised that He will always be with us in the fiercest storm to see us safely through. It is one thing to know this intellectually, but quite another to know it experientially. Britt writes out of experience, and thus has proved thorough his own experiences the faithfulness of God, which makes this book authentic not just in theory but also in actual practice.

Pastor Chuck Smith
Pastor, Calvary Chapel of Costa Mesa
Costa Mesa, California

I have written many books about spiritual breakthrough. It is something we all want. In *Big God*, Britt Merrick shows us a key to all spiritual breakthrough: simply having faith in a big God. Thank you, Britt.

Elmer Towns
Author of *Fasting for Spiritual Breakthrough*

BIG GOD

BIG GOD

WHAT HAPPENS WHEN WE TRUST HIM

BRITT MERRICK

Regal

From Gospel Light
Ventura, California, U.S.A.

Published by Regal
From Gospel Light
Ventura, California, U.S.A.
www.regalbooks.com
Printed in the U.S.A.

Library of Congress Cataloging-in-Publication Data
Merrick, Britt.
Big God : what happens when we trust him / Britt Merrick.
p. cm.
ISBN 978-0-8307-5222-5 (hard cover)
1. Faith. 2. Faith—Biblical teaching. 3. Bible. O.T.—Criticism, interpretation, etc. I. Title.
BV4637.M438 2010
234'.23—dc22
2009049650

1 2 3 4 5 6 7 8 9 10 / 15 14 13 12 11 10

Rights for publishing this book outside the U.S.A. or in non-English languages are
administered by Gospel Light Worldwide, an international not-for-profit ministry.
For additional information, please visit www.glww.org, email info@glww.org, or write to
Gospel Light Worldwide, 1957 Eastman Avenue, Ventura, CA 93003, U.S.A.

This book is dedicated to my wife, Kate,
who has taught me more about the beauty, bigness
and love of God than anyone. I love you.

When she speaks, her words are wise,
and she gives instructions with kindness.
PROVERBS 31:26, *NLT*

CONTENTS

ACKNOWLEDGMENTS

I would like to thank my parents, who first taught me that God was bigger and more valuable than anyone or anything else. Because of them, I have had the desire to follow Christ into mission. That mission has been particularly shared with an amazing group of people known as "the staff" of Reality Carpinteria and Ventura. They have brought me so much love and friendship, and without their work I never could have completed this work. I look forward to many more years of pursuing faithfulness and fun for God's glory with all of you.

A huge thank you to Bill Denzel at Regal who really made this book happen and in whom, through this process, I have gained a great friend. To my fellow church planter Pastor Dave Lomas of Reality San Francisco who, while training under me to plant a church in that amazing city, spent many fun and fruitful hours with me in the study discussing Hebrews 11. Thank you—this book is yours, too.

I must also lovingly acknowledge my children, Isaiah and Daisy, who make my heart sing and constantly teach me about God. Finally, to the congregations at Reality Carpinteria and Ventura: We discovered and labored over and rejoiced in these truths together. This is your book. I love all of you and consider it the privilege of a lifetime to be called "pastor" by you.

PREFACE

In each of our lives, we have moments in which we must make significant decisions that can change the path of our journeys. This book is about those choices and people who have made them. These are people we've read about before but may have never really considered how significant their choices were—both to them and to all of us people of faith who look to their lives as examples of God's faithfulness. This is about their trust and the big God they put their trust in. Through these stories we see that He was worthy of their trust, their faith. And He is worthy of our trust today.

WHEN MY HEART IS OVERWHELMED

Hear my cry, O God; attend to my prayer. From the end of the earth I will cry to You, when my heart is overwhelmed; lead me to the rock that is higher than I. For You have been a shelter for me, a strong tower from the enemy. I will abide in your tabernacle forever; I will trust in the shelter of Your wings.

PSALM 61:1-4, *NKJV*

I MUST CONFESS THAT MY HEART WAS OVERWHELMED during the writing of this book. You see, during the days and nights I was going into the depths of faith as lived out long ago by some of our Bible heroes, my little five-year-old daughter fought cancer. When this book went to press, I didn't know if the cancer had been completely eradicated. At the time she was in the middle of chemotherapy and radiation treatments.

What I do know—what I am absolutely certain of—is that my God is big, and He is worthy of my faith. My God is a big God, who held my daughter in her hardest moment and holds her now. He also clasps my family and me in the palm of His hand. Nothing is too hard for Him. This trial with my daughter's health has already shown me how God grasps and sustains me in ways that I never thought possible. Let me tell you the story.

Monday Morning

Because I'm a pastor, Monday is my day off. My wife, Kate, and I enjoy spending those days together. This particular Monday, we really needed some rest and relaxation. It had been a busy summer but finally the kids were back in school. Kate and I planned one of our surf dates. We don't have many "date nights," instead we have "date days" so we can go surfing when the kids are in school.

As we prepared to head to the beach, I got a call from Daisy's school. The caller said, "Daisy's fallen down and she doesn't look good. She's having a hard time staying conscious." We found out later Daisy had vomited and knew something was wrong. She told the lady caring for her, "You need to call 911. I need to go to the doctor." Daisy falls all the time so the concern over this little fall didn't make sense. Nonetheless, my wife and I rushed to Daisy's school, grabbed her and took her to the emergency room.

Immediately, the doctors could tell that something was very wrong. They examined her and thought she had ruptured her spleen. Suddenly things got a lot scarier and more intense. An attendant shouted some serious sounding medical jargon and before we knew it a whole army of doctors and nurses poured into the room. Kate and I were quickly ushered out. We could see on the faces of these emergency room professionals that the situation was bad. After a quick ultrasound, they did a more extensive CAT scan that showed a huge mass in Daisy's abdomen. The doctors thought it was probably a bunch of blood, and that she might have ruptured a kidney. They moved Daisy from the emergency room to ICU, and the doctors worked diligently for a definite answer.

After we had been in the ICU awhile, one of the doctors finally told us, "That mass we're seeing in Daisy's abdomen is not blood; it's a tumor. And it's about the size of a Nerf football."

The tumor went from down inside her pelvis bone, all the way up to her diaphragm, and was pressing against her lungs, taking up more than 50 percent of her abdominal cavity. The doctor said, "We're going to try to figure out what this tumor is right away." So they connected her to a number of machines. And all Kate and I could do was wait with Daisy. And pray.

A few hours later, one of Daisy's doctors found us and dropped the bomb. "Well, we think that your daughter has cancer. We think it's a Wilms' tumor and it's the biggest one we've ever seen here. And we're going to have to operate."

Those words were some of the hardest I've ever had to hear. My head reeled. My heart ached. My little girl had cancer. In an instant, our world had been radically changed.

All we could do was wait for the operation, which was scheduled three days later on Thursday morning. It was still Monday, and all they could do was care for her in ICU. As we spoke with the surgeon, he said, "You know, this tumor is really big. And the surgery is going to be complicated because the tumor is near the vena cava and the aorta, which are the blood supplies that come down and then fan out. And it's all around. It might be connected with some organs."

The surgeon didn't seem very confident that he would get it out. So Kate and I started praying. Our family began to pray. As we got the word out, our entire church started praying. Daisy's story spread on the Internet, on Twitter, by word of mouth, and people and churches all around the world began to pray for her.

Thursday

Daisy was wheeled into the operation room at 7:15 A.M. About six hours later (an eternity when you're waiting), the doctors and nurses emerged with the news that, miraculously and wonderfully, they had removed the whole tumor. We had a moment to celebrate that, but when we spoke with the surgeon afterwards, he told us the tumor had been hemorrhaging and leaking cancerous cells into her body, which meant that her cancer was considered at stage 3.

A biopsy confirmed the mass to be a Wilms' tumor, which is highly treatable with a high cure rate. They also told us we would face seven months of chemotherapy and radiation. The first chapter was over, but the rest of the story had yet to unfold.[1]

When Crisis Hits, Where Do Your Heart and Mind Turn?

What do you do as a Christian when the doctor tells you that your five-year-old daughter has cancer? How do you deal with that? If you're a Christian, your mind goes to Jesus. That's just where you go. As soon as I heard "Your daughter's fallen and she's not doing well," my mind went to Jesus. As soon as I got to the emergency room and they said, "We think it's this . . . we think it's that," my mind went to Jesus. When the doctor stood before me and said, "It's the biggest tumor we've ever seen of this sort, and we think it's stage 3 cancer," my mind went to Jesus.

Why is it that Jesus is the first thought that comes to mind? Why do we run to Him? What informs our thought processes in these times

---

1. For an update on Daisy's progress, you can visit http://prayfordaisy.tumblr.com.

of life? My experience with Daisy has sharpened my understanding that what shapes the way we handle crises is the Book we as Christians base our lives upon—the Bible.

Our minds took a certain route to Jesus when we first heard the news. We went *through the Word of God*. Immediately our hearts and our minds were filled with truth we had learned from the Bible, and an understanding of the character of God. Immediately our hearts and minds were filled with the story of God and how He has proven Himself faithful with His people over and over again, since the beginning of time. Immediately our hearts and minds were filled with the Bible's stories of people just like you and me who faced problems, and placed their little bit of faith in a big God.

"I Have Hidden Your Word in My Heart"

Precepts and passages came quickly. And we didn't even have to open the Bible. We didn't need someone to come along and quote Scripture to us. It was just there, because we had done one simple thing in life: we had committed to reading our Bibles. It's like Colossians 3:16 says: "Let the Word of Christ richly dwell within you." The Word of God is living and active,[2] and it's supposed to interact with us at these times of life. The Word was immediately a comfort,[3] a lamp, a light[4] and an instructor.[5] Because we had read our Bibles, we could fall back on His truth, His promises and what we knew about His character. And that's what protected us from the schemes of Satan.

I don't know if we always realize how wicked Satan is, and how intent he is to ruin our lives. He will seize upon every opportunity he can. He has no sympathy, no mercy, no compassion and no shame. When the doctor told us that our little baby had cancer, Satan would have loved to come

2. Hebrews 4:12.
3. Psalm 119:50.
4. Psalm 119:105.
5. Psalm 119:97-99.

in and whisper lies in our ears, to cause doubt and anguish. But the Word of God was like a shield against the schemes of the enemy.

In addition to the attacks of Satan, we also face the simple pitfalls of the flesh—all those places your mind and emotions want to go. But when the Word of God dwells in you, it will begin to control and shape your thought processes and emotions. When we faced this trial, the Word of God came over us like a flood. We were covered by passages such as Philippians 4:6-9:

> Be anxious for nothing, but in everything by prayer and supplication with thanksgiving let your requests be made known to God. And the peace of God, which surpasses all comprehension, will guard your hearts and your minds in Christ Jesus. Finally, brethren, whatever is true, whatever is honorable, whatever is right, whatever is pure, whatever is lovely, whatever is of good repute, if there is any excellence and if anything worthy of praise, dwell on these things. The things you have learned and received and heard and seen in me, practice these things, and the God of peace will be with you.

As they came to us, verses like this shaped and protected our hearts and our minds, and prevented us from going to the dark places. We began to think about the resurrection of Jesus Christ and His resurrection power. And we remembered Paul speaking about sharing in his sufferings.[6] We recalled the book of Hebrews, where we learned that we have a sympathetic high priest who is touched by the feelings of our infirmities, who is there, who is near and who cares about us.[7] This is what protected Kate and me at the moments when our hearts were overwhelmed.

---

6. Philippians 3:10.
7. Hebrews 2:17-18; 4:15-16.

The Word of God Brings Life

Psalm 61:2 says, "When my heart is overwhelmed; lead me to the rock that is higher than I" (*NKJV*). Jesus is that rock. And the way we are led there so often is through the Word of God. As Psalm 119:25 says:

> My soul cleaves to the dust;
> revive me according to Your word.

In the worst moments of life, when I don't know how to get off the floor, God's Word does something in me that brings me back to life. Psalm 119:28 reinforces this thought:

> My soul weeps because of grief;
> strengthen me according to Your word.

There is strength that is drawn from God's Word in the bitter moments of life. It is supernatural and otherworldly, because it is the Word of God. Again, we see this in Psalm 119:50:

> This is my comfort in my affliction,
> that Your word has revived me.

I want to testify that this is truth. As Kate and I went through what were absolutely the worst few days of our lives, the Word of God revived us time and time again. We frequently stood on Psalm 119:162:

> I rejoice at Your word,
> as one who finds great spoil.

Knowing God's Word, believing it and standing on it, prevented us from groping around like a lost soul in the dark. Being committed to a life of knowing the Word of God helped us through those heartbreaking moments.

Don't Forget to Feed On the Word

Here's the secret: when our hearts are overwhelmed, it is best to have already fed on the Word of God. If a person hasn't been reading the Bible, it's never too late. We can always choose to be in it. Choose to believe it. Choose to trust.

We need to intentionally *choose* to trust in the Word. I know that there are difficulties with the Bible, but there are also plenty of reasons to believe that it is the living, actual, true, trustworthy Word of God. Just because there are some difficulties doesn't mean that we cease to trust. Like everyone, I have had some struggles in my marriage, but when my wife tells me that she loves me, my mind does not immediately go to, *Yeah, but you love chocolate, too, so what does love really mean?* That would just be silly and wrong.

When the Word speaks to us, even though we struggle with some passages, we don't immediately think, *Well, I don't understand all of it, so I don't trust it.* I know that some "theologians" are going there. I know that some seminaries have gone there. I know that many in the Church in America are going there. But don't go there. The Word of God is living, active, inerrant, infallible, authoritative and true. As A.W. Tozer once said (and I paraphrase), "We can't expect those without faith to understand the power of the Word because it is through faith that the Word is revealed."

Have it in your heart and have it in your head. Let the Word of Christ dwell richly in you. Because when someone looks you in the eyes and says your five-year-old daughter has a cancerous tumor the size of a Nerf football, you better know some Bible. Not for the sake of the Bible itself, but because the Bible tells us about Jesus, and reveals the character of God so that we can know that He is good and faithful.

Feed Upon the Stories

I'm only in my thirties, so I've barely lived long enough to know how faithful God can be. But when I read the Word of God, I see thousands of years of history. The Bible shows me that God is faithful through the stories of men and women who experienced His faithfulness first-hand. It's those stories that protect and help us. We can feed upon those stories when we need strength.

The psalms as well helped to protect us. In Psalm 62:5-8 we read:

My soul, wait in silence for God only,
For my hope is from Him.
He only is my rock and my salvation,
My stronghold; I shall not be shaken.
On God my salvation and my glory rest;
The rock of my strength, my refuge is in God.
Trust in Him at all times, O people;
Pour out your heart before Him;
God is a refuge for us.

The first prayer that my wife and I said out loud as we waited there in the emergency room was a passage right out of the psalms. My mom had just arrived and it was the first time that we had a chance to hold hands and pray together. And what we prayed was directly from Psalm 91:1-2:

He who dwells in the shelter of the Most High
Will abide in the shadow of the Almighty.
I will say to the LORD, "My refuge and my fortress,
My God, in whom I trust!"

We just said, "God, we trust You. We trust You right now with our daughter's life. You give and You take away. Whatever the outcome of this is, we want to say that we trust You, God." I don't think I would have known how to say that unless I had already been nourished by the Word of God. We remembered the next verses in Psalm 91:3-4:

For it is He who delivers you from the snare of the trapper
And from the deadly pestilence.
He will cover you with His pinions,
And under His wings you may seek refuge;
His faithfulness is a shield and bulwark.

Because we had read the Word of God, we knew we could hide
under the wings of God. We knew to cling to the person of Jesus.
We knew that metaphor. We understood God's character and knew
that His faithfulness would be a shield for us. It was His word that
nourished us, like good food when your body is sick. As Psalm 37:3
says, "Trust in the LORD and do good; dwell in the land and feed on
His faithfulness."

Don't Wait Until You Need It

Now is the time to feed on the faithfulness of God. Just like a little
lamb that is out in the pasture, you have to feed. He is our shepherd
and we are the sheep of His hand. How do you feed but on His faithfulness? We do that by being in the Word of God and knowing the stories, so that when the famine of hard times comes, we have the food
that will sustain us. Believe me, each of us will face difficulties in life.
When we do, we will also experience His faithfulness personally—if we
have been in the Word of God.

As we anxiously waited for Daisy to be seen by the doctors, the
Word of God reminded us that God is in control; Isaiah 55:8-9 came
to mind:

"For My thoughts are not your thoughts,
Nor are your ways My ways," declares the LORD.
"For as the heavens are higher than the earth,
So are My ways higher than your ways
And My thoughts than your thoughts."

We're simply not going to understand when a five-year-old has cancer. Especially when it's yours. But then we remember that God is in control. He doesn't promise us understanding. He promises us peace beyond understanding.[8] The Word of God reminds us that God is good and that He cares. One verse that my wife held closely during that first week was Psalm 56:8. In this verse, the psalmist says to God:

You keep track of all my sorrows;
You've collected all my tears in your bottle.
You've recorded each one in your book (*NLT*).

Why Ask Why?

All of these verses, all of these precepts, all of these truths, were already in us when we received the worst news of our lives. And that kept us from going to that place of asking God, "Why?" I want to testify that by the grace of God we never asked why, because the Word of God doesn't necessarily give us the whys. His ways are higher than our ways. "Lean not on your own understanding," Proverbs 3:5 says (*NIV*). The Word of God always told us that. And it kept us from an unhealthy trap of asking "Why?" or "Why me?" The why questions only lead through a long and winding maze of "How could You do this?" to "Don't You care?" to "Can I believe Your Word?" and inevitably to "Can I believe in the character, cross and resurrection of Christ?" Where would that leave us?

Having been fortified by the Word of God, we never had to ask why. We simply always said, "We trust You, God." I don't say that to boast. I say that to encourage you. It didn't require any great faith because we had read our Bibles and knew that our God was a big God whom we could trust, no matter what. That is what gave us a foundation, a solid footing when it seemed as if the world crumbled around us.

---

8. See Philippians 4:7.

Where Faith Comes From

Having a foundation in the Word allows us to deal with God when He doesn't heal. That's where the faith to carry on comes from. Faith comes by hearing the Word of God.[9] We asked God to heal Daisy, and thousands of people around the world have prayed for her healing. I completely believe that God is able to remove tumors in an instant. I know people who no longer have tumors—God removed the growths. I have faith to believe that God can do it again—and we asked Him to. I held my little five-year-old in my arms and said, "God, just take the tumor away. You can do it in an instant; it's nothing for You. You raise the dead. She's not dead. You can do this!" And He didn't do it.

The reality is that it takes more faith to endure Christ not healing your daughter than it does to see Him heal her. And I would rebuke anyone who says: If God doesn't heal you, there must be some deficiency in your faith. Are we to say that the five-year-old little girl who was lying in that hospital bed had a deficiency in her faith and so God refused to heal her? Is that what we learn from the Word of God? It is not. That idea comes from the wicked heart of man. God is able to heal at all times. But He doesn't. If anybody ever had faith it was the apostle Paul, but God didn't heal him. In fact, God said expressly, "I will not heal you. My grace is sufficient for you."[10]

Christ was not healed—He died on the cross. If Christ should suffer and die, why would we think we should not? If God would let His own Son be tortured and nailed to a cross, who are we to think God is wrong if He lets our children die of cancer? Is the life of my daughter more precious than the life of Christ or the lives of the thousands of children who are dying at this moment in obscurity, without emergency rooms and wonderful surgeons and thousands of people praying for them by name? We sometimes esteem the life of men too

---

9. See Romans 10:17.
10. See 2 Corinthians 12:7-10.

highly—even over the Word of God and the person of Christ. For the Church it should be a delight to share in the sufferings of Christ so that we might know the glory of Christ and the power of His resurrection. And if He would take our babies today, we would see them in glory tomorrow. We don't grieve like the unbelieving world, because we know in Whom we have placed our trust. When David's little baby died, he got up and washed himself and ate. And he said, "I will see that child again."[11]

It Is Good

Pondering that Scripture as I prayed for Daisy, I was reminded of Psalm 119:71:

> It is good for me that I was afflicted,
> That I may learn Your statutes.

This may seem a weird place to go, and I experienced some tinges of guilt when I went there, as Daisy was in the hospital. I've been able to hold the hands of my wife and say this to her, not as a preacher or a pastor, but as a parent and a partner: "This is good for us." We don't rejoice in cancer, but the Bible tells us that we have a God who is bigger than cancer, who is more valuable, more wonderful, and who has given us a resurrection. So we're able to say, "It is good for me that I was afflicted so that I may learn Your statutes."

Until we experience affliction, all these truths are merely theoretical. I confess that many of the things I've read and preached and taught have been theoretical. It doesn't mean I don't believe them. I do completely and absolutely, just like I believe in gravity. But when you jump out of an airplane, you believe in gravity in a different way. In that moment it becomes a lot more real.

---

11. See 2 Samuel 12:19-23.

I can't tell you how often I've quoted and taught Romans 5:3-5: "But we also exult in our tribulations, knowing that tribulation brings about perseverance; and perseverance, proven character; and proven character, hope; and hope does not disappoint, because the love of God has been poured out within our hearts through the Holy Spirit who was given to us." But I never experienced it like I did when Daisy was diagnosed with cancer. Until that time, I really didn't know what tribulations were, other than the time my wife and I lost a child in a miscarriage.

Kate had been pregnant for about four months and we were making plans for life with a new baby—our second child. At the same time, we looked forward to the launch of the new church called Reality in Carpinteria, California. Kate had a miscarriage one week before the church was to open its doors. That was six years before our crisis with Daisy. Ironically, we launched Reality Ventura, a satellite campus of the church, two weeks before we discovered Daisy had cancer. One day as we waited for Daisy to come out of surgery, Kate looked at me and said, "You know, every time we start a church, it seems like it costs us a kid."

I don't know the heart or mind of God and I don't know if those things are connected or not, but I do know that Jesus said that if we're going to follow after Him, we've got to count the cost.[12] I know Paul taught us not to consider our lives more precious than the person of Christ, and to esteem everything else as rubbish in light of knowing Him.[13]

And so these concepts are coming out of the theoretical and becoming real. And what I discovered in the midst of this trial is the beautiful truth that I really do know Jesus. And that's exactly where we want to be, ultimately.

Do You Know Him?

Let me challenge you with this question: Do you really know Him? Maybe you are going through the motions. Maybe you're religious.

---

12. See Luke 14:25-33.
13. See Philippians 3:8.

Maybe you show up at church and sing a few worship songs, but you don't know Jesus. Let me encourage you to get to know Him. Is He a tower of strength and a refuge for you? Is He the first place you go? Is He your ultimate comfort? Your highest goal? Your greatest desire? If not, do you really know Him?

Each of us can ask ourselves if—like the psalmist—we want to dwell in His tent forever and take refuge in the shelter of His wings.[14] Walking by faith is not easy, especially when dealing with something that affects your child. There's a reason Jesus gave us the commandment that we shall have no other gods before Him. It's because we have a proclivity toward having other gods. We have a tendency to find more satisfaction, joy, pleasure and excitement in things other than the person of Jesus. But when your world is rocked by a significant trial, those things just kind of get shaken loose and begin to fall away, and what's left is the solid foundation, which is, hopefully, Jesus. If you don't have Jesus when those trials come, you'll find yourself left with nothing and no solid place to stand.

Love Him More than Anyone or Anything

As I walked through this trial with Daisy's health, one of the surprising things that happened over and over is that my spirit erupted in worship. My heart would suddenly break out into worship of God and who He is—not always out loud, but always real. I don't say that to boast. I say it to testify that Christ is more wonderful than any other person or relationship. My mom taught me at a very young age that she loved God more than she loved me. (I'll tell you the full story in chapter 6.) That affected me profoundly. It helped to keep me from creating idols out of certain relationships.

We've taught our kids the same thing. I can't tell you how many nights I've put Daisy to bed and said, "I love you, Daisy. Daddy loves

---

14. See Psalm 61:4.

you more than anything in the world." She always corrected me, "Nuh-uh, Daddy. Not more than God. You love God more than you love me. And I love God more than I love you."

That's the most wonderful thing you could ever hear as a Christian parent. Part of the corrupted human side of us feels a cutting when we hear our children say, "I love God more than you." Part of us worries about what our children might think when we tell them that we love Christ more than we love them. Yet this is the first and greatest commandment. If we fail in that one, we're failing in all of them. I have been tested in that as I walked through this illness with Daisy.

Are you obeying that first and greatest commandment, the one found in Deuteronomy 6:4-6?

> Hear, O Israel! The LORD is our God, the LORD is one! You shall love the LORD your God with all your heart and with all your soul and with all your might. These words, which I am commanding you today, shall be on your heart.

Jesus echoed this in the New Testament when He said, "Love the Lord your God with all your heart and with all your soul and with all your mind. This is the first and greatest commandment."[15] That has been tested in my life. In the furnace I discovered if that was really true.

There comes a time when Jesus has to show up on your beach in the midst of your stuff and say, "Peter, do you love Me more than these?" He went to Peter's beach on the north end of the Sea of Galilee, confronted him right in the middle of his world and restored him with the simple question, "Do you love Me more than these?"[16] And the text doesn't tell us what "these" are. It leaves it ambiguous so that we might always think that "these" means everything. Jesus Christ showed up on my beach that day in the midst of my stuff and said, "Britt, do you

---

15. Matthew 22:37-38, *NIV.*
16. See John 21:15-17.

love Me more than these?" Immediately Psalm 63:3 came to mind: "Your love is better than life" (*NIV*).

Putting Daisy on the Altar

Wednesday night, the day before Daisy's surgery, I had my dark night of the soul. I had to say goodbye to Daisy. So many people had faith the surgeons would get the whole thing. I had faith too, but God didn't let me go there. God had me with Daisy all night long. In the middle of the night, He stepped back onto my beach, like He did with Peter thousands of years ago, and asked me a simple question: "Britt, do you love Me more than these?" I said to Him that night, "God, if You let my daughter die tomorrow, nothing changes between me and You. Nothing changes between us, Jesus. I will yet praise You. You give and You take away; blessed be Your name. I love my little baby, God. But I love You more. And I trust You. I don't need to understand. I trust You implicitly."

Take a moment to examine your life today because your life's circumstances could be very different tomorrow. Make sure Jesus is number one. Read your Bible. Remember the stories. Place your faith in our big God, because He is worthy. He is the God that keeps track of our sorrows and stores up our tears in a bottle. He is more faithful than we will ever know, more wonderful than anything else in life, more desirable than anything this world has to offer. His loving kindness is better than life.

FOR AS LONG AS I CAN REMEMBER, my father, Al Merrick, has been respected in the surfing world as a world-class surfboard shaper. He has made boards for many of the world's greatest surfers, including multiple-time world champions Tom Curren and Kelly Slater. He is recognized as an innovator in the sport, and has even had documentary films made about him. But one of the greatest honors he has received was being inducted into the Surfers' Hall of Fame in 2007. Very few have been given this honor, and even for a humble and self-effacing man like my dad, it was a big deal. Having him officially recognized as one of the best sealed what all of us already knew.

Nearly every field of endeavor has a hall of fame. The Bible has its own version, found in Hebrews 11—the chapter that has become known as the "Hall of Faith." In Hebrews 11 we are given reminders of a number of men and women who had great faith at critical moments in their lives. Retold through the ages and across many cultures, their stories are truly remarkable, certainly worthy of Hall of Faith status. But if you look closer, you'll see the heroes of these stories aren't necessarily great people. They had good days and bad days—and most of them had enough bad days that they could have just as well been placed in the "Hall of Shame," if there were one. But at the pivotal moments of their lives, when it really mattered, they had faith in a great God they knew and trusted.

In the next chapters, we will walk through their stories one by one. We'll see that these were real people with real lives and real problems, like you and me. Faith is a real life issue. As we study the faith decisions these men and women made, we'll be encouraged to continue to grow in faith and to press on toward maturity.

That could be a goal you set: to mature in your faith as you learn and understand the lives of people of faith from Scripture. Hebrews 6:12 says that we are not to be sluggish as it pertains to growing, but "imitators of those who through faith and patience inherit the promises." So when it comes to our Christian growth, we shouldn't be sluggish—we should be fervent. One of the ways that we can do that is by imitating the men and women found in Hebrews 11: Abel, Enoch, Noah, Abraham, Sarah, Moses, Rahab, David, and others.

The Definition of Faith

To understand how to grow in our faith, we must have a grasp on what faith is. We are given a definition of faith in Hebrews 11:1: "Now faith is the assurance of things hoped for, the conviction of things not seen." In the *New American Standard Bible,* which I use most, the words can be a little confusing. (At least, they were confusing to me.) The *New International Version* makes better sense of this verse: "Now faith is being sure of what we hope for and certain of what we do not see."

The *New Living Translation* provides another excellent translation of this key verse: "Faith is the confidence that what we hope for will actually happen; it gives us assurance about things we cannot see." Faith is confidence and assurance. The *Contemporary English Version* also translates this verse well: "Faith makes us sure of what we hope for and gives us proof of what we cannot see." The *New Century Version* says, "Faith means being sure of things we hope for and knowing that something is real even if we do not see it." That's good: knowing something is real, even if we don't see it. All these versions help us to understand this complex idea of faith a little bit more.

The Basis for Our Faith

Put very simply, faith is trust. When discussing faith in the context of Hebrews 11, we're talking about a particular sort of trust, not the kind based merely on knowledge. That's not to say that kind of trust is brainless or blind, because it's not. And that's not to say it doesn't involve any knowledge at all, because it does. It's just that the *primary* basis for this trust, this faith, is not so much *what you know* but rather *what God has said.* That's the issue. Hebrews 11:1 clearly describes faith as involving things that have not yet happened (things hoped for), and things that we cannot see. Because they haven't happened and because we cannot see them, it can be difficult to base our trust on knowledge. So this trust, this faith, is based on what God has said and done, not on what we know empirically or what we have seen with our eyes.

Faith must be based on the revelation of God's character, His track record and His written Word. When we build on these things, our faith makes the future immediate and the unseen tangible. Future truths concerning our Christian faith and the work of God become present and powerful in our daily living, and unseen realities become actual and able to be seen, through the eyes of faith.

Faith Failures: Adam and Eve

While our goal is to look at faith heroes we can imitate, it's also help-ful to consider a few key faith failures, starting with Adam and Eve. If we think of faith as trust and consider what trust is to be based upon, we realize that it isn't knowledge when we look at Adam and Eve's story. To begin with, they didn't really have any knowledge they could draw upon. I mean, God created them as adults, so they must have had a certain amount of knowledge, but they were literally new. Think about it. They were brand new, so what could they know?

I had a friend that I used to spend a lot of time with, a Jewish Christian pastor friend. Whenever I would do something stupid—which apparently was often when we hung—he would say in his Jew-ish accent, "What are you? New?" Well, Adam and Eve were literally new. What did they know? Not much, but they were in relationship with God and they had God's spoken word. So it was upon that foun-dation that their trust in God was to be made. And in God's economy, in God's mind, that should have been enough to cause them to trust him. God said, "From any tree of the garden you may eat freely; but from the tree of the knowledge of good and evil you shall not eat, for in the day that you eat from it, you will surely die."[1] Now, what did

---

1. Genesis 2:16-17.

they know? They didn't know anything. So if they were going to trust God's statement, the only thing they could base their trust on was relationship and what God said.

What we saw in the Garden was distrust. They didn't trust God. They knew Him. They had a relationship and they had His Word. That should have been enough for a trusting relationship and for them to do the right thing. But for some reason it wasn't.

A Solid Foundation

Hebrews 11:1 says, "Faith is the assurance of things hoped for." It could also be translated "the substance of things hoped for." In this context, that word "assurance" or "substance" in the Greek has the idea of "foundation." Assurance, or substance, is the foundation of our Christian hope. So faith is to Christianity what a solid foundation is to a house. It gives us confidence that we will stand. It gives us confidence that we are secure. It gives us confidence that we can remain. Faith is the foundation of the Christian life. And for any foundation to be reliable and meaningful, you have to know what it's made of, right? It really matters what your foundation is made of. That makes all the difference in the world

In Matthew 7, Jesus talked about two different types of foundations. The first was built on the sand, and the second was built on the rock. Jesus said, "Don't build your house on sand, because when the storms come it's going to erode and your house is going to fall. Build your house on the rock."[2] Jesus used the metaphor of building a house on a rock to communicate the spiritual truth that our lives are to be built upon the solid, unchanging and eternal foundation of the Word of God. Those who live on or near a beach know building right on top of sand is not a good idea. He used a common idea that people could understand: a sure foundation is needed. What is your foundation made of?

---

2. See Matthew 7:24-27.

For faith to be meaningful, it has to have an object, a sure foundation. That foundation is Jesus Christ. Faith built on something other than itself is a silliness that has beset much of Christianity. You've heard of this deception: name it and claim it, blab it and grab it. The names are as ridiculous as the belief itself: *If I just believe enough, it'll happen.* As if faith were some unperceivable, intangible, powerful force that can *make* God do things. That's not what faith is. We're not talking about having faith in faith itself, nor are we talking about the common mantra among even secular humanity that says, "You just gotta have faith, bro." I'm sure you've heard that one too. Remember the song? "You just gotta have faith, you just gotta have faith." Well, that's utter nonsense. "You just gotta have faith." Faith in what?

We can place our faith—our trust—in the foundation and focus of our faith: Jesus Christ and the promises He has made.

Why We Can Trust Jesus

Now the power behind any promise is the person that made that promise. Think about it. There are certain people in your life who will say, "Oh, I promise," and it means nothing to you. Sure, they said the magic words: "I promise." But the words are meaningless because you knew the person behind that promise.

There are other people in your life that when they say, "I promise," you know you can take it to the bank. You know that person is reliable. They have a good track record of keeping their promises to you and other people. You can trust them. The power behind any promise is the person who made the promise.

The power behind the promises of Christianity is the person of Jesus Christ. That means that all the things the Bible speaks of—all the things our faith speaks of—can be trusted. Has He ever failed? Has He ever not made good on His Word? Has He ever not come through?

Even though sometimes it doesn't seem like it, He has been absolutely faithful through the generations. You may have dramas in your life that didn't work out the way that you wanted, but don't blame that on God. Sometimes you make your own messes. He warned us that because of sin in this world, we would have trouble.[3] But He is still faithful. He is absolutely faithful and his track record proves it.

In 2 Corinthians 1:20, Paul says, "For all of God's promises have been fulfilled in Christ with a resounding 'Yes!'" (*NLT*). This means all the good things that God has promised us as His people are sure to happen because of the person of Jesus Christ. As sure as Jesus came and is coming again, we can count on God's promises being fulfilled in and through Him. So when we talk about the future hope and we talk about faith, we're talking about Jesus. We are putting our faith, our hope, all in Jesus.

Now when we *do* examine evidence that is tangible, knowable, perceivable, concerning the Christian faith, we reaffirm that faith in Jesus Christ is both reasonable and founded. Our faith is not blind. It's not brainless. It's not based on a mere feeling. We're not talking about a hunch. It's not an *Oh, I hope so* sort of thing.

Faith in Jesus Christ is not sentimental. Nor is it merely an intellectual assent to certain doctrines. Faith in Jesus Christ is a solid conviction because it rests on God's Word, which makes the future present and the invisible seen with the eyes of faith. Now the problem with the original recipients of the letter of Hebrews—the reason the letter was written to them—is that they were caught up in the here and now, in the difficult circumstances of the moment. They lived in a time in the Roman Empire when Christianity had been declared an illegal religion. Because of this, they experienced great persecution and were sure to experience more.

Their devotion to Christ was not turning out the way they had expected. It had brought them some real trouble—and now they were beginning to rethink that spiritual commitment and relationship in light of their physical circumstances. These pressing things were

---

3. See John 16:33.

wholly consuming them, driving their emotions and causing their faith to waver. For you, life may be all about what is happening right now—the immediate, the tangible. But the Bible says that faith is the conviction of things *not* seen. And that word "conviction" in the Greek means proof or evidence.

Believing Is Seeing

Proof, or evidence, of things not seen. Now that's an oxymoron. At the very least, it's a strange dichotomy. The world says that seeing is believing. We hear that all the time. "Show me." "Let me see it." "I'll believe it when I see it." That's what the world says. But the Bible says, "Hold on! Wait a minute. There's something more than meets the eye." In fact, it says that "the righteous shall walk by faith and not by sight.[4]

The reality is that there is an unseen realm, a spiritual world, and that world impacts our lives every moment of every day. When we walk in awareness of this world, with a conviction of its reality, we walk with a "certain resolve of certainty." We walk knowing the spiritual truths the Bible declares are indeed true, even though we can't see them in the physical. For example, in the book of Hebrews we are told that the priestly ministry of Jesus Christ is an ongoing ministry. He acts on our behalf and for us. Now I don't see it, here in the physical. We don't *see* Jesus doing the priestly ministry but the Bible declares that it is ongoing, that it's happening, that it impacts our lives. Hebrews 7:25 tells us that "He always lives to make intercession" for us, meaning that He bears the wounds which won and testify of our salvation before the Father day and night.

We don't *see* Jesus interceding for us, but we definitely believe that it happens. We experience the temporal benefits of it as well. So when I mess up, when I sin, Jesus is pleading the cause. He's standing before the Father. He's bearing the wounds. He ever lives to make interces-

---

4. My paraphrase. See Habakkuk 2:4; Romans 1:17; Galatians 3:11; Hebrews 10:38.

sion, to testify that the cost of my sins was covered at the cross.[5] Now that's a truth. We believe that even though we don't see it.

Likewise, our direct access to God in prayer is another absolute truth we believe but can't see. The book of Hebrews tells us that we have access, that we can enter into the Holy of Holies to come before our God.[6] There's no veil in the temple that separates us from the presence of God. There's no ark. There are no cherubim on the mercy seat visible to us. We can't see God's presence and His availability to us in prayer, but we absolutely believe it and we rely upon it daily.

I don't know about you, but I rely daily upon the ability to approach the Throne of Grace with boldness so that I may receive mercy and help in the time of need. I rely on the fact that I can go and be in the presence of God to gain new strength, to develop character and to simply enjoy Him. I can't see it, but I count on it. It impacts my daily life.

Another spiritual reality we experience is the full pardon of sins. We can't see it, but we certainly believe it. The Bible declares that we have the conviction of things not seen,[7] that our sins really have been moved as far as the east is from the west,[8] buried in the deepest sea,[9] dealt with once and for all,[10] and that God chooses to remember them no more.[11] You do not have visual evidence that your sins have been dealt with. You didn't put them in a big trashcan that was taken to the dump and emptied out. You didn't throw them into a fire and watch them burn up. But even though you didn't see it happen, you believe that your sins are removed and gone.

We also believe that God is in control and that He's on the throne. And while this is an *unseen* reality, it is absolutely sure. I have the conviction that God is on the throne even though I don't always see it in

---

5. See Colossians 2:14.
6. See Hebrews 4:16; 10:19-22.
7. See Hebrews 11:1.
8. See Psalm 103:12.
9. See Micah 7:19.
10. See Hebrews 10:10.
11. See Isaiah 43:25.

the circumstances of the world. We may be at war, or experiencing a troubled economy. Families are broken, and perversion is rampant. So when I look at the situation in the world, I don't always see God on the throne, but the Word of God tells me that He's on the throne.[12] And I've read the end of the Book. Guess what? It comes out okay.[13] He really is on the throne, ruling and reigning and working. Don't give up. The story's not over yet. God is in control.

The Future Trumps the Moment

I imagine that on the day Pontius Pilate gave the command to crucify Jesus, many Christ-followers in Jerusalem thought that was the end of it. They probably thought the Pharisees had won. They probably thought Rome had won. They probably thought perhaps even the devil had won.

But the verdict of the future reversed the verdict of the moment. In the moment, in the immediate, it seemed all things were lost. Some followers of Jesus left town and were heading for Emmaus, heartbroken and crestfallen. But the verdict of the future—the fact that Jesus Christ died on the cross to pay for the sins of the world and after three days rose again victorious over sin, death and the devil—reversed the verdict of the moment. For this reason Christians must have a heart set on hope—of the rapture of the Church, of His second coming, of His just judgment, His establishment of the millennial kingdom, a new heaven, a new earth, a new Jerusalem, the hope of God residing among His people.

We hold these things as absolute truths of which we are convinced. These truths help life to make sense, because the verdict, or promise, of the future overwhelms and reverses the verdict of the moment, what we see with our eyes. That's faith. That's trust and that affects the way

---

12. Revelation 4.
13. See Revelation 19-21.

we live. When we consider that future hope as we make decisions in the here and now, we are empowered to forego the momentary passing pleasures of sin for a weightier eternal reward.[14] That's what we do as Christians. We do some things—and don't do other things—because of what we believe about the future. The world says, "Well, why should I refuse the pleasure of the moment for an uncertain future?" But we are certain there's a future in Christ that is better. We believe in a heavenly reward and in a just judgment. Those beliefs affect our behavior.

At the time of its writing, more than 25 percent of the Bible was prophetic in nature. So in the macro, the future is absolutely certain—and that's because it is in the hands of God. Read the end of the Book if you're not quite clear. He wins.

Faith Affects the Way We Live and Die

Our faith is a dynamic certainty about what God has said and what God has promised, based on His character track record. Faith has to do with what we believe about the past, the present and the future and this affects the way that we live *and* the way that we die. Hebrews 11:13, speaking of the men and women of faith that we'll study in the following chapters, says, "All these died in faith, without receiving the promises, but having seen them and having welcomed them from a distance, and having confessed that they were strangers and exiles on the earth."

They died trusting what God was doing and trusting what God had said, but yet never receiving the promises—even though they did see the promises with the eyes of faith and welcomed them from a distance. Having seen them in this way, their faith made the invisible visible. Their faith made the future a present reality, so they "confessed that they were strangers and exiles on the earth" because their reality transcended what they experienced in the physical realm. They looked forward with eyes of faith to the fulfillment of promises in the life to

---

14. See Hebrews 11:25.

come. They lived as citizens of God's kingdom rather than any kingdom on earth. Their trust in God transcended what is tangible, visible and visceral.

When God Calls You Out

So the Hebrew Christians were told the forefathers came and they persevered in faith. They died in faith. They laid hold of the invisible with the eyes of faith. They acted on the future by living a life of faith. They are the example. "But," the writer tells the Hebrews, "you have now experienced the salvation of Jesus Christ, His cross and His resurrection, so you had better live by faith, move forward in faith and not try to return to the place God brought you out of." As he says in Hebrews 11:14-15, "For those who say such things [referring to their confession that they were strangers and exiles on the earth] make it clear that they are seeking a country of their own. And indeed if they have been thinking of that country from which they went out, they would have had an opportunity to return." What the writer of Hebrews is speaking of is the fact that these Hebrew Christians were tempted to return to Judaism because of the persecution they were experiencing as Christians. He's saying all of these great stories of faith were people coming out of someplace. And if God calls you out of something, He is faithful to provide a way out.

In my own life I was called out of a lifestyle of drug use and sexual immorality. I'll admit that life seemed good at the time, but I sensed—I knew—that God was calling me out of that life and into something better. When I finally decided to obey, I discovered that God provided all the strength I needed to get free from habits, addictions, and unhealthy relationships. And, perhaps surprisingly, I discovered that life was more fun and much better walking with Jesus than living a life that testified against the reality of my faith in Jesus. Later, God would call me out of something that was *very good* to bring me into something *even better.*

Abraham was called out of Ur of the Chaldees by God. He had to leave it all behind and just go. Noah had to leave some things behind. So many of these great stories of faith are about God taking us to new places. The writer of Hebrews tells us in Hebrews 11:14-15 that if your mind is always set in and stuck on the past, you'll be in trouble. He told the Hebrews to leave those things behind and press on: "Let us press on to maturity."[15] "Press" is an action word. Growing in your faith is active. In Philippians 3:13-14, Paul says it well: "Brethren, I do not regard myself as having laid hold of it yet; but one thing I do: forgetting what lies behind and reaching forward to what lies ahead, I press on toward the goal for the prize of the upward call of God in Christ Jesus."

Trust Through the Tough Times

Following Jesus into the next season of your life is going to require greater faith, so you have to take stock of where you are now. Are you pressing on or are you just maintaining the status quo? Are you stuck in a rut? Is your heart set on the here and now, or are you looking forward, in faith and trust, to the promises of God? Hebrews 11:16 says, "But as it is, they desire a better country, that is, a heavenly one. Therefore God is not ashamed to be called their God; for He has prepared a city for them." And Colossians 3:1-3 urges us to set our hearts and minds on the things above, where Christ is, rather than on the things that are on earth.

We need to look forward to what God has said He will do. We need to be people of faith, confident and ready for the future. Hebrews 11:6 says, "And without faith it is impossible to please Him, for he who comes to God must believe that He is and that He is a rewarder of those who seek him." Without faith, without trust, it is impossible to please God.

Our heroes in Hebrews 11 exercised moments of great faith and were approved by God because of their faith, even though they had numerous failures. Hebrews 11:2 says, "For by [faith] the men of old

---

15. Hebrews 6:1.

gained approval." They pleased God. Again, if you were to take the whole of their lives, they could just as easily be in the Hall of Shame. For every great moment of faith, they endured several failures in faith. And yet, because they had faith at pivotal times, at the critical moments, they gained approval with God. They pleased the Lord simply by trusting Him.

Are you trusting God? Faith and trust really matter when adversity comes and challenges happen. That's when we are tempted to not trust. We often don't even know that temptation is there until adversity hits. Then, all of a sudden, we experience a real deep-seated distrust toward God. That's exactly what Adam and Eve discovered in the Garden. They should have—and could have—trusted, because of relationship and because of what God said. But in the moment, in the face of deception, they failed to trust. True Bible faith is confident obedience to God's word in spite of circumstances and consequences. That was the message to the Hebrews. At that moment, they were being threatened for believing in Jesus Christ. Some of them, in the future, would have their lives taken from them. So the writer of Hebrews is encouraging them, telling them to continue to trust Jesus, no matter what it costs. That's the crux of our faith. No matter what it costs, Jesus is trustworthy. No matter how difficult it is, no matter how much the opposition, we must continue to trust Jesus. And for the Hebrews the cost was huge. It would cost them property and position and reputation and even their very lives, and yet the word to them was, "continue to trust."

How Faith Works

To break it down, faith operates simply in one clear order: God speaks. We listen. We trust him. So we obey him. It's that simple. That's how faith works. When it really matters is in the face of adversity, challenges, difficulties and hard circumstances. But no matter how difficult or uncomfortable, no matter what the consequences, we continue to obey. The outcome may be unknown and the obstacles large, but we trust God's ways and His methods and do what is good and right. That's the life of faith. Our circumstances may not be like the circumstances of those first-century recipients of this letter. The consequences may not be as extreme, but to you and me they are just as real.

We all make faith decisions every single day in every area of our lives. Do I trust God with my finances? Am I listening to what God says about tithing and stewardship? Do I trust God with my recreation? With sobriety? Do I trust God with my business? Am I walking in honesty and integrity? Do I trust God with my relationships? Am I following the Bible's direction on reconciliation, forgiveness, extending mercy and grace? Do I trust God with my heart? With my emotions? We must make faith decisions that show whether or not we trust Him in every corner of our hearts.

This is the life of faith. What the Christian endeavors to do is to trust God, and trusting God pleases God. Without faith it is impossible to please God. Who are you trying to please in this lifetime? If it's God, you're going to make good faith decisions. If it's not Him, you're bound to make some bad decisions. In the next chapters, we'll meet a few people that you've heard of before—some you'll remember from stories you heard and songs you sang in Sunday school. You will be surprised to learn their full stories are a lot more intense than you may have been told. We will look at their lives as examples of faith, of trusting God with incredibly hard decisions. Their faithfulness through those times made them pleasing to God and carried them through what would later be recognized as some of the most pivotal moments in history. These are their stories. Imitate them and find the reality of faith.

I LOVE LITTLE HOUSE ON THE PRAIRIE.

It's one of my all-time favorite old-school television shows. I love watching it with my family. We have all the DVDs. On occasion there are some good faith lessons in there, too. Sometimes they really mess it up, but overall, it's good.

I watched an episode one time with my kids in which Pa Ingalls was working really hard to grow the crops, just like he always did. You know, it was hard to make it living out there on the frontier. So the crops were all planted, and had started growing. One night as the family was sleeping, violent cracks of lightning and claps of thunder awakened Pa. He looked outside, and there was a huge hailstorm just hammering his crops. So he threw on his hat and his jacket and ran out to the field. Ma Ingalls started to pray right there in the house. Mary peeked through the window, and little Laura tried to get around her to see her Pa out there in the middle of the night trying to save the crops. Finally, he came in just before dawn and gave the family the bad news. He had lost the whole thing. He had worked for months to grow those crops. Months. Then in one night, their livelihood was lost because of a single storm.

What would you do in this situation? Would you complain? Become depressed? Throw something at a wall? Or would your first thought be to worship God? Yes, I suggest that we should turn to God with gratefulness. How does that work?

Our life of faith begins with worship. In fact, A.W. Tozer states that it is the purpose for which we were created. So it fittingly follows that one of the best stories we have of faith shown through worship comes at the beginning of the Scriptures, in Genesis. It's the account of Abel, the first of the "heroes of faith" listed in Hebrews 11.

Abel's story of great *faith* comes on the heels of the great failure of Adam and Eve. Ironically, Adam and Eve's failure was a failure of faith. And, get this, a failure to trust. They were in relationship with God, and they had God's Word, and that should have been enough for them to trust. But they didn't. They took matters into their own hands. They didn't trust God or His Word.

That third chapter of Genesis can be somewhat disheartening. Especially after that great creation account, at the end of which God looks at everything and says, "This is good. This is very good."[1] It seemed like we were off to such a good start. Then Adam and Eve come along and make a big mess—just because they didn't trust the Lord.

But born from the depths of that momentous failure, one of their kids, Abel, had a great moment of faith. This first example of an authentic life of faith has to do with how we worship. You can take that as a cue. The fact that the very first story of faith is about how we worship tells us that worship is very important to God. That means it should be very important to you and me as well. In fact, worship is the *most important* thing. Why? Because it is in worship that God is glorified, and we exist to glorify God. We were made by God and we were made for God.[2] Then we rebelled, we distrusted, we mistrusted, and we fell away from God. But God is a missionary God, so He sent His Son Jesus Christ to save us and to restore our relationship with Him. He came and draped Himself in humanity and lived a perfect life because we couldn't. He died an atoning death on the cross so that we wouldn't have to pay the price for our sins. And He rose from the dead to give us brand-new life. When we accept, understand and receive that, by faith we enter into new life. Then we realize that our lives are no longer our own and we are not allowed to live for our own glory anymore.[3]

We Live to Worship

We are to pursue and live for God's glory above all. That means that selfishness, self-absorption and the self-centered, egocentric patterns and tendencies must be left behind, repented of and forsaken. Worship becomes everything and everything becomes worship.

---

1. See Genesis 1.
2. See Colossians 1:16.
3. See 1 Corinthians 6:19-20.

When we see people *not* living for God's glory, we long to tell them about Him and His renown. We respond with what we call missions or outreach. In *Let the Nations be Glad!* John Piper writes, "Missions exist because worship doesn't."[4] We do missions for God's glory so that worship can rise up where now a void exists. We share the gospel so that humanity might be redeemed, and so that redeemed people of all nations will adore and exalt Christ. We want all people to find and fulfill their life's purpose by worshiping their Creator because we know this simple fact: it is to worship Him that we were created.

Where Authentic Worship Begins

When we look at these great stories of faith in Hebrews 11, the first one—the story of Abel—has to do with how we worship, how we relate to the glory of God. Not *how* in regard to the position of your body, but *how* as in the position of your heart. Have you ever noticed that the Bible has very little to say about worship's form or style or liturgy? That's a good thing. The Bible says that we ought to worship, but it says very little about *how* we ought to physically worship. And that's good, because people are different. From church to church, worship can look totally different and still glorify God.

So when we talk about how we worship, we're talking about the condition of your heart. That's the crux of it. Worship is an issue of the heart and a matter of faith. Worship is only authentic when the heart is authentic, when your heart is truly yielded to, subsumed by and consumed with God and His glory. To live a life of worship like that takes faith. And trust. If worship and the glory of God are the most important things, then you and I, as God's people, should always seek to bring our best before God when we worship Him. That is something that should be a no-brainer to the redeemed mind. Now

---

4. John Piper, *Let the Nations be Glad!* Second Edition (Grand Rapids, MI, Baker Academic, 2003), p. 17.

that takes more faith than you might imagine, as you'll see in the story of Abel.

Our Decisions Display Our Faith

In the Christian life, everything we do must be done by faith, with an attitude of trust in God, in order to be pleasing to Him. Our decisions must display the fact that we trust God. We need to begin to think in terms of trusting God with our identity, with our relationships, with our money, with all the stuff that we do and have. Quite simply, faith is trust, and we make faith decisions every single day, in every area of our lives. We make faith decisions about our finances, about our sexuality, about our recreation, about our business, and about our relationships. We also make faith decisions about our hearts, beginning with whether or not we're really going to trust God with all of our hearts. All these things require daily decisions based on trusting God, according to who He is and what He has said—decisions not merely based upon knowledge, but rather upon who God is, His character and what He has said in His Word. We can only please God in these various aspects of our lives if we're trusting God with them. If we don't trust the Lord in these areas, then we're not pleasing the Lord.

Abel pleased the Lord, and as a result we have this story, this model of faith. Hebrews 11:4 says:

> By faith Abel offered to God a better sacrifice than Cain, through which he obtained the testimony that he was righteous, God testifying about his gifts, and through faith, though he is dead, he still speaks.

So here we have this little important verse about Abel. It says that Abel offered to God a better sacrifice than Cain. A better sacrifice. Think about what Abel did. His was just a simple act of adoration. A work of worship. The timing is significant. His sacrifice came *before* the law existed. The Levitical law had not yet been given at Sinai. God hadn't yet told His people: When you sin this way, then you need to sacrifice in this way. So this was not a sacrifice of penance, or of atonement. It wasn't a sin offering or any of those things. It was simply an unsolicited, authentic act of adoration—a work of worship that flowed from the heart of Abel.

The "More" Sacrifice

So then why is it called a sacrifice? Looking at the definition of "sacrifice" helps us to understand. Sacrifice is defined as an act of giving up something valued for the sake of something else regarded as more important or worthy. A sacrifice must first be something of value, something that we believe has worth. It must be something we give up because there is something or someone of *greater* value.

Both Abel and Cain brought a sacrifice in the story, but Abel offered a *better* sacrifice than Cain. The Greek word used here for "better" is *pleion*, and it means "more." A good translation is that Abel offered a "more sacrifice." Not more in quantity, but in quality. Qualitatively speaking, it was a more sacrifice. The *New American Standard* translates that word as "better." It was a better sacrifice. The *King James* and the *New King James Versions* add the word "excellent." They say it was a "more excellent sacrifice," but in the Greek, the adjective "excellent" isn't there. Finally, the *English Standard Version* and the *New Living Translation* add the word "acceptable" to say "a more acceptable sacrifice," but that adjective isn't there in the Greek either. The only adjective used is *pleion*. Abel offered a "more" sacrifice. Remember that.

Based on this act of adoration, this sacrifice or gift that Abel brought to Him, God's assessment of the man was that he was righteous. Now, it's true both in the Old Testament and the New Testament that one is only made righteous by faith.[5] God has never changed

---

5. See Genesis 15:6; Ephesians 2:8.

the way that He saves people. He always saves people by faith. But Abel's sacrifice was an act of faith, and God declared Abel to be righteous because of it. In fact, Jesus refers to Abel in Matthew 23:35, calling him "righteous Abel."

So it wasn't merely the gift itself, the *thing* that Abel gave, it was the heart behind the sacrifice that made it acceptable to God. It was the attitude of the man that caused him to be "reckoned righteous" by God. But some questions still remain: Why was Abel's sacrifice better and why was it by faith? And, more practically, what is the story of faith here that we can imitate? Let's look at the original story in Genesis 4:1-7:

> Now the man had relations with his wife Eve, and she conceived and gave birth to Cain, and she said, "I have gotten a manchild with the help of the LORD."
>
> Again, she gave birth to his brother Abel. And Abel was a keeper of flocks, but Cain was a tiller of the ground.
>
> So it came about in the course of time that Cain brought an offering to the LORD of the fruit of the ground.
>
> Abel, on his part also brought of the firstlings of his flock and of their fat portions. And the LORD had regard for Abel and for his offering; but for Cain and for his offering He had no regard. So Cain became very angry and his countenance fell.
>
> Then the LORD said to Cain, "Why are you angry? And why has your countenance fallen? If you do well, will not your countenance be lifted up? And if you do not do well, sin is crouching at the door; and its desire is for you, but you must master it."

When Cain expresses anger in this situation, it becomes evident that there is something in his heart that isn't quite right. So the Lord calls him on it and gives him a warning: "Cain, what's going on in your heart? Watch out! Sin is crouching at your door and its desire is for you." That word "desire" in the Hebrew is *teshuqah*, and it means here a desire to exercise authority or control over. God tells Cain, "Sin's desire is for you, but you must be master over it." But Cain didn't listen when the Lord warned him about sin crouching at the door. He didn't hear when God said that sin wanted to seduce him and bring him into a destructive lifestyle, a destructive pattern of living. He didn't heed the Lord, so he fell into temptation; he killed his brother. Genesis 4:8 says:

> Cain told Abel his brother. And it came about when they were in the field, that Cain rose up against Abel his brother and killed him.

While Satan may be the father of murder, Cain is its human inventor; he commits the first murder in all of history. Something has gone terribly awry in the heart of Cain, very shortly after the fall of man. It's reflected in his actions and in his worship. Returning to Genesis 4:3-4, it's very clear how different Cain's worship was from Abel's:

> When it was time for the harvest, Cain presented some of his crops as a gift to the LORD. Abel also brought a gift—the best of the firstborn lambs from his flock (*NLT*).

Giving Your First

This is where it all hinges, and it really is a big deal: Abel brought from the *firstlings* of his flock. In Christianese or in Bible-talk, we often say "from the first fruits." But what is a "firstling"? The *Oxford American Dictionary* defines it as "the first agricultural produce or animal offspring of a season." It is possible that this was not only the first offspring or crop of the season, but perhaps the very first time that Abel's flocks had ever given forth children, and the first time that Cain had ever had a harvest.

Genesis says that Abel brought of the firstlings of his flock. Notice that it does not say the same about Cain and what he brought. He simply brought some of the harvest. The Holy Spirit is very intentional about the words that are used—and are not used—in Scripture. Cain brought some of his harvest, but Abel brought the *first fruits*, the firstlings of his. That is the difference between Cain's and Abel's sacrifices. It is not that one was agriculture and the other livestock.

Both types of sacrifices would be deemed acceptable to God when the Levitical Law was later revealed. Rather, it was the condition of their hearts and the priority they gave or did not give to God in their sacrifices. While this is the first mention, subsequently throughout Scripture God's people are encouraged to bring their first fruits before Him. It is the idea of giving your best to God and it is symbolic of the whole life of worship and all that that entails.

Faith Gives God Priority

Bringing our very best before God requires faith. It requires trust. And the reasons it does are threefold. First, it gives God priority. It's an act of faith and trust because it says that God comes first. Isn't it true that the first thing you choose to do in a situation says a lot about your heart? Remember those commercials? "Hey, you just won the Super Bowl. What are you going to do next?" And the response was "I'm going to Disneyland!" (or "Disney World" on the East Coast). As if at this great moment, right after this great accomplishment, the first thing on this athlete's mind—just bounding forth from his heart—is an intense desire to hang out with Mickey Mouse. That's his priority? Those ads ring false because what you put first reveals the priorities of your heart.

In reality, it is true that what you give priority to—what you put first—reveals, betrays and exposes your heart. It's just that simple. The first thing that you do, your default, your go-to, really shows what's in your heart. Abel's act in Genesis 4 of bringing his first fruits before God revealed what was in his heart. He gave God priority, and this expression of faith pleased God. It also landed Abel a place in Hebrews 11 as one of the examples for us to imitate as we live a life of faith. In Abel, we see a life that puts God first and gives God priority in the totality of life. As Christians, we are not called to compartmentalize our lives. They're to be laid open before God so that He can be the Lord of our whole lives. He's to have priority, which means worship comes first in every area of our lives.

Faith Is Trusting God for the Rest

The second reason Abel's act required faith is because he trusted God for the rest. Raising sheep was his livelihood—that which kept him and his family alive—and what would happen for Abel after he sacrificed his firstlings was an unknown. That's the key. He had to trust the Lord for the rest because there's always that unknown element to the future. When you bring your offering, it's gone—out of your hands, out of your control. Faith has to do with the future and the unseen, and when we bring our first to God, it means we are trusting Him for the rest of it.

The world says, "Wow, you're riskin' it, dude!" But in life with Christ, it's trust. We're trusting God to provide the rest. So we bring our first to the Lord with confidence. You never know when recession is going to hit. You never know when your paycheck is going to decrease or go away. So, giving of the first fruit really is an act of faith, an act of trust, to give to the Lord.

Faith Is Contrary to Human Nature

The third reason Abel's sacrifice required great faith is that it was against human nature. You see, human nature is self-preservationist, right? We have this "watch out for number one" attitude. I've got to look out for *me*. I've got to make sure that *I'm* okay, that I get my portion, and *then* we'll talk about everything else. So giving the first to the Lord, trusting Him with our first fruits, is contrary to human nature.

Because after all, human nature is basically greedy, isn't it? We tend to play it safe and try to preserve ourselves, instead of trusting God to take care of our needs. That's why Abel's sacrifice was an act of faith: on the surface, it didn't appear to be safe. It went against human nature.

If you have a self-preservationist mindset, then maybe you give later. If you're greedy, then maybe you never give at all. But a person of true faith gives. They give the best to God, they trust God for the rest and that mindset goes against human nature. Proverbs 3:9 tells us exactly what we are to do:

> Honor the LORD from your wealth
> And from the first of all your produce.

That's how we are to worship: by giving our finances, our wealth, our stuff. The Scripture doesn't say "give from the leftovers." It says "from the *first* of all your produce." The next verse gives us a promise:

> So your barns will be filled with plenty
> And your vats will overflow with new wine.

That is an accompanying, conditional promise. *If* you honor the Lord from your wealth, giving God priority, *then* your barns will be filled. If you trust Him for the rest, He will be faithful to provide it. Scripture makes the promise that when we honor God with the first of our produce, He will take care of the rest. Your barns will be filled with plenty and your vats will overflow with new wine. Many people can't live that way. That way of life is counterintuitive. Those who live without faith might say, "Well, let me fill up my barns first and then we'll talk about what we have left."

So in the story of Abel we see this concept in Scripture of giving our first to God in worship. And we now understand why that was a matter of faith. It was giving God priority, trusting God for the rest and contrary to human nature.

Giving in Daily Life: God or an iPod

What does this concept look like practically for you and me in our daily lives? Well, let's take a very simple example of tithes and offerings. Let's not beat around the bush. Giving to the Lord in tithes and offerings is a normal part of the Christian life as laid out in Scripture. We give directly to God and it is meant to be an act of worship. We can't miss that. When we give our tithes and offerings at church, it is meant to be an act of worship. It is part of the worship service. It's part of the liturgy. It's part of the service of the church. When we come to church, we come to worship. We worship by enjoying God. We worship by loving one another and experiencing the love of God. We worship in song, we worship by studying the Word of God, and we worship by giving. Throughout Scripture, giving is meant to be an act of worship. If that attitude of worshiping God by giving is not in your heart, then you are in error. When the bag, or the plate, or the bucket, or whatever you use at your church comes around, and you choose not to worship by giving, you're making a mistake. Hey, that's not my opinion; it's just what Scripture says!

What would it mean today to bring your first fruits before the Lord? Well, practically speaking, it would mean that when you get your paycheck and you sit down to write your checks and pay your bills, the first check you write is to the Lord. But back in the time of Abel, they didn't have checks; they had crops and animals. And the first of those crops or animals was to be given to the Lord. It was always the first. That is the act of faith. So when your first check is to the Lord, that's an act of faith—especially in these times. It's an act of faith because it gives priority to God in a very practical way. I think it does something in the heart of a man or a woman when they sit down with a pile of bills on one side and a little paycheck on the other side and say, "Well, the first check is going to the Lord." The tithe, which means 10 percent, and the offering, which means giving that's above and beyond the tithe—whatever you give—is going to the Lord *before* you deal with the bills. That's practical, pragmatic, and consistent with Scripture. It also requires faith, because who knows what's hidden in the bills these days.

What *isn't* faith is to pay all the bills, buy all your stuff and then say, "Oh, I have a little bit left over. I'm going to take that to church on Sunday. Going to give that to the Lord, a little leftover here. Here You go, Jesus." You know what? Better to just keep it. It wasn't an act of faith. And without faith, it's impossible to please God. There is no trust in that—it was your leftovers! Better to go get yourself another iPod or something. Because your giving doesn't please the Lord unless it's an act of faith. I mean literally, when a man or a woman sits down and says, "I don't know how these finances are going to add up, but I'm giving first to the Lord." In Malachi 3:10, the Lord makes a promise to those who give. It's the only time in all of Scripture that God invites us to test Him:

> "Bring the whole tithe into the storehouse, so that there may be food in My house, and test Me now in this," says the Lord of hosts, "if I will not open for you the windows of heaven and pour out for you a blessing until it overflows."

What a great promise. And what a bummer to miss out on that promise of God, to not experience that life of faith, that act of worship.

The Offering of Time

Let's take another simple example: our time. There's an easy one. You know, time with God is meant to be the worship of God, and we are called to spend time with God. We know that, right? The cross happened that we might be reconciled in relationship. Any relationship you have where you don't spend time together is not going to be a great relationship. If I'm never home with my wife and I show up for dinner and just scarf and scram, there's not going to be much relationship there. If I don't spend any time with my kids, we're not going to have a good relationship. Relationship is predicated upon and dependent upon time spent together. The Christian life, the life of worship, the life of faith, requires that we spend time with God.

So how do we find the time to spend with God? We give it priority, put it first, and trust God for the rest of the time to get our other stuff done. And that's counterintuitive, because most of us would say, "I don't have enough time!" Martin Luther had this down. He is known to have said that he was so busy, that he had so many things to do, that he had to spend the first three hours of the day in prayer. He gave God first dibs on his time. He trusted God with all the things he had to do and he went against human nature that says, "Got to go, got to go, got to run and git'r done!" Instead, he said, "So many things to do today, I've got to spend the first three hours with the Lord." And if anyone accomplished something significant in his or her lifetime, it was Martin Luther.

Who or What Is Your God?

Two things are the most telltale in our lives: finances and time. You can tell everything you ever wanted to know about peoples' hearts, passions and priorities from the way they spend their money and the way they spend their time. You simply cannot argue with that. If the priority in their finances is themselves and the priority in their time is themselves, then they are their own god. If it's cars and guitars and surfboards and similar things, then those are their gods. As Christians, our God is Jesus Christ, so our money and our time must be prioritized accordingly. We see an illustration of this in Mark 12:41-44:

> And [Jesus] sat down opposite the treasury, and began observing how the people were putting money into the treasury; and many rich people were putting in large sums. A poor widow came and put in two small copper coins, which amount to a cent.[6] Calling His disciples to Him, He said to them, "Truly I say

---

6. These small copper coins were the least valuable Jewish money in circulation at the time.

to you, this poor widow put in more than all the contributors to the treasury; for they all put in out of their surplus, but she, out of her poverty, put in all she owned, all she had to live on."

Now I want you to notice that Jesus was there in the temple observing how people were giving money. Not how in the sense of the physical form of payment—debit or credit, cash or check—but how as in their hearts. Scripture says that God looks upon the heart of a man.[7] He was observing how they were giving by watching their hearts, their attitudes. But notice how He discerned their hearts: He does it by looking at the way they handled their finances. He says in Mark 12:43 that the poor widow put in *more*. There's the same Greek adjective that we read in Hebrews 11:4, *pleion*, more. The poor widow gave a "more" sacrifice, just like Abel. She put in more than all the others who gave greater amounts.

Why did Jesus call it the "more sacrifice"? Because it required faith. You see, that was all she had. Many commentators say that was all she had to live on for the day. If you understand first-century Judaism in the social context, you know that life was very difficult for widows. Their income and how they ate and were provided for was very sketchy in that day. That's why the mandate in the New Testament is to visit widows and orphans in their distress; they needed help.[8] But this widow, in faith, gave everything that she had to live on for that day. Not just the first fruits, but also all her fruit. God just asks for the first fruit, but she gave all the fruit. That's a great story of faith. The others, it says in Mark 12:44, gave out of their surplus. They gave their leftovers! They had plenty and said, "Okay, I'm covered, and now I've got a little bit left. I'm going to the Temple. I'm going to give it to the Lord." Although the widow's gift was very, very small quantitatively, qualitatively it was more; it was *pleion*. Jesus said,

---

7. See 1 Samuel 16:7.
8. See James 1:27.

in effect, "This woman has done it right. She has given more than everybody else."

Bring Your Best, Not the Rest

And this teaches you and me that as we worship with every area of our lives, we're to bring our best to God. That's what we need to take away from this story. We need to bring our best before the Lord and not our leftovers. I don't know how we got this way as Christians, but somehow it seems like Christianity has become this realm of leftovers. It's weird. We give God our leftover time. We give Him our leftover money. When the church has a rummage sale, we give our leftover junk that nobody else will take. I find it disheartening that so few Christians today are really making Jesus the priority of their lives. Having been created by God for the glory of God, having once rebelled against that and then been redeemed by the Son of God, by the blood of Jesus Christ, we as Christians now exist for His glory, and not for ourselves. We are not our own. We've been bought with a price. Therefore, we are to glorify God in our bodies, as Paul says in 1 Corinthians 6:19-20. We are to bring our best before the Lord.

The widow's sacrifice was authentic worship and not mere religion because it required so much trust for her to give it. The other guys in this story, the rich people, just gave out of religion. They brought some of their leftovers to the temple to give to God. That's religion. That's what a lot of people do. How about you? In your finances, are you making faith decisions? Even in tough financial times, it's essential to do finances with faith. Where do you put your trust? Hopefully not with the government or Wall Street. The only sure thing is to put your faith—financial decisions and all—in Jesus Christ, the one who will never fail us. He deserves to be worshiped with every area of your life. And, let's be honest, money is a big part of our lives. It is for me. Isn't it for you? So, if you're not worshiping with your finances, there's a huge part of your life that is void of worship—and that's not good.

The Heinous Subplot

Any time somebody endeavors to live out authentic worship in their lives, they're going to encounter opposition. Cain opposed Abel because of his "more" sacrifice. As you know, Cain wasn't too happy, so he killed his brother. Opposition doesn't get much worse than that. We see opposition emerge again, in a less dramatic yet poignant way, in Mark 14:3-9:

> While [Jesus] was in Bethany at the home of Simon the leper, and reclining at the table, there came a woman with an alabaster vial of very costly perfume of pure nard; and she broke the vial and poured it over His head.
>
> But some were indignantly remarking to one another, "Why has this perfume been wasted?
>
> For this perfume might have been sold for over three hundred denarii,[9] and the money given to the poor." And they were scolding her.
>
> But Jesus said, "Let her alone; why do you bother her? She has done a good deed to Me.
>
> "For you always have the poor with you, and whenever you wish you can do good to them; but you do not always have Me.
>
> "She has done what she could; she has anointed My body beforehand for the burial.
>
> "Truly I say to you, wherever the gospel is preached in the whole world, what this woman has done will also be spoken of in memory of her."

Jesus didn't say that about anybody else in Scripture. That's not said about Abraham, that's not said about Jacob, not about David, Caleb, Joseph, Joshua, Daniel, Isaiah, Peter, Paul or John. The *only* person in history that Jesus said that about is this woman, Mary of

---

9. Three hundred denarii was about 11 months' wages at that time. This lady just poured 11 months' wages on the head of Jesus in worship!

Bethany. Wherever the gospel, the good news about Jesus, goes forth, the story of what this woman Mary did shall be spoken of in memory of her. From that we begin to discern what is important to God. You see, worship takes priority over everything else. This was an authentic act of worship before Him. This is what excites the heart of God. By making that statement, Jesus is clearly saying, "This is a better portion. This pleases me. This is the way that you want to be."

Mary's act pleased the Lord because it was lavish, enthusiastic and sacrificial. It wasn't reserved—there was life and passion in it! Believe it or not, the sacrifice cost her eleven months' wages. How's that for an act of giving up something valued for the sake of something else regarded as more important? This act of faith pleased the Lord.

And guess what happened next? She faced immediate opposition. Mark does not tell us here, but John tells us in his gospel that it was Judas. Judas is the one who said, "What, what, she—what?! We could have sold that for money!" John 12:6 tells us why Judas is concerned:

> Now he said this, not because he was concerned about the poor, but because he was a thief, and as he had the money box, he used to pilfer what was put into it.

Judas, repelled and offended by authentic, sacrificial, enthusiastic worship, raises his opposition. Beware of that heart. Be ready for it. Expect that opposition when you truly give the Lord priority in your life.

Don't Be a Judas

Going back to Mark 14, in verse 10, Judas displays what was really in his heart: "Then Judas Iscariot, who was one of the twelve, went off to the chief priests in order to betray Him to them." It stands to reason that if you don't worship God in your finances, you might betray Him with your finances. That's the dichotomy and the choice that emerges here. Will you be self-serving or self-sacrificing?

Judas was self-serving. Mary was self-sacrificing. Hers was an act of faith because it gave God priority, it trusted God with the associated costs, and it was contrary to human nature. And wherever the gospel goes forth, what Mary did will be spoken of as a testimony to her faith. That's similar to what Hebrews 11:4 says about Abel. It says that he "obtained the testimony that he was righteous . . . and through faith, though he is dead, he still speaks." You see, for the righteous man death is not the end. In fact, for every man death is not the end. All of our lives will speak when we are dead. Something will be said. It might not be much. It might be great. It might be awesome. And this is Abel's testimony: Because of a simple act of worship filled with faith and trust, he pleased God and was considered righteous.

What is your testimony? I mean if people look at your time and your finances, what will they learn about you? And when you die, if people are honest—and at funerals they seldom are—what will they say about you? I've officiated funerals that were wonderful celebrations of the person's life of faith. I actually enjoy those. But I've done others where nobody came. I've been to funerals where nobody had a good thing to say. In the end, everyone's life has something to say. How will your life speak?

What God Wants

In Romans 12:1, Paul says this:

> Therefore I urge you, brethren, by the mercies of God, to present your bodies a living and holy sacrifice, acceptable to God, which is your spiritual service of worship.

Now we're talking about the ultimate sacrifice: just giving our whole lives. Presenting your body means giving your whole life to God.

One Saturday morning, I sat on the couch in my house before dawn, studying these passages about the life of faith. My little daughter, Daisy Love, who was four years old at the time, woke up early and came running out to see me. She came out in her Chonies with her pink blanket, teddy bear and messed-up hair. She jumped into my lap and started snuggling. She could tell that I had my mind on something because I was looking at the computer screen and had my Bible and a few books open. She's seen me study a lot, but this morning she asked, "Daddy, what are you doing?"

I said, "Well, sweetheart, I'm studying to teach the Bible tomorrow at church and to talk to people about Jesus."

"Oh? What are you going to talk about?"

"Well, we're talking about faith and giving our best to God."

Her response blew me away. "You mean like yourself, Daddy? Because the only thing that God wants is you. God doesn't want your money or your things. The only thing that God wants is you. Is that what you mean, Daddy?"

At age four, she got it. I'm not sure how, but she got it!

You see, we've been considering our finances because that's where this story takes us. But God doesn't want your money. He wants your heart. The problem is, our hearts get all wrapped around money. That's why God deals with our pocketbooks. In doing so, He's really dealing with our hearts. And our time is just as problematic. These things—our money and our time—are matters of faith in which we ought to give God priority. We need to give Him our best, trust Him for the rest, and live the lives we were meant to live, walking with supernatural power and flying in the face of human nature and the world's wisdom. Because that's what pleases Him: those simple acts of faith that show we trust Him with everything. After all, He just wants us. So we offer ourselves up as living sacrifices. But the only problem with living sacrifices is that they have a tendency to crawl down off the altar. So if you've been running, getting out of that place of giving God priority, return to His heart. Show Him you trust Him with everything. Put your faith in the One who deserves it.

4

FAITH WALKING

Enoch

*By faith Enoch was taken up so that he
would not see death; and he was not
found because God took him up; for he
obtained the witness that before his
being taken up he was pleasing to God.
And without faith it is impossible to
please Him, for he who comes to God
must believe that He is and that He is a
rewarder of those who seek Him.*

HEBREWS 11:5-6

OUR SECOND INSIGHT INTO GREAT FAITH IS REVEALED through the story of Enoch. In Hebrews 11:5, we learn that Enoch was pleasing to God and that he was taken up to be with God. That's all the information we are given. Not a lot, for sure. However, whatever the details, it's easy for us to glean this fact: Enoch had great faith because the testimony of his life pleased God. As Hebrews 11:6 says, without faith it is impossible to please God, so even with such few details, we do know that Enoch had great faith and pleased God with his life.

Let's go hunting for more about Enoch. In Genesis 5, we discover that he came seven generations after Adam. Genesis 5:21-24 says:

> Enoch lived sixty-five years, and became the father of Methuselah. Then Enoch walked with God three hundred years after he became the father of Methuselah, and he had other sons and daughters. So all the days of Enoch were three hundred and sixty-five years. Enoch walked with God; and he was not, for God took him.

There's not a lot more information here than what we're given in the book of Hebrews. But there is something very powerful in this passage: the statement that Enoch *walked with God*. Two times it says Enoch walked with God. Since it's mentioned twice, there must be something here. What faith lesson are we to learn from the fact that Enoch walked with God?

Next Steps in the Life of Faith

Abel shows us *where* the life of faith begins, but Enoch shows us *what* the life of faith consists of. Enoch walked with God. That's about all we know. But we understand the concept, because the phrase "walking with God" is part of our Christian grammar. If I'm to sit down with a guy for accountability or discipleship, I'll often say to him, "Hey, bro, how's your walk?" I'm not asking him if he has a limp or if he has some sort of interesting stroll. I'm asking him how his relationship with the Lord is going. It's common language for us.

Let's try to put legs to the idea of "walking with God." Why does this phrase require faith, or trust? What was Enoch's deal? Why is it so profound? Why was his walk with God such a great display of faith? Well, let's start by looking at what the word "walk" signifies.

First, when we think of walking, we think of a *voluntary act*. It says that Enoch "walked" with God, not that Enoch "was dragged" by God. Second, walking signifies a *steady* motion. It doesn't suggest a stuttering start/stop action, nor does it mean to run hard, run fast and then just kind of poop out. Third, walking signifies *progress*, a continuous, forward traveling. That's what walking is. So that simple word, "walking," makes us think of a voluntary act that moves us forward at a steady pace. We can begin to see why walking serves so well as a metaphor for a progression in spiritual things.

So, if it is a voluntary act, then to walk with God means to live a life that is *surrendered to God*—a life of saying, "Not my will be done, but Your will be done, God." Walking with God also means living a life that is *controlled by God*. It's steady and reliable. And finally, a walk with God means a life that is *lived for God*. It speaks of discipleship and progression. It suggests a life that is lived for God's glory, God's purposes, and God's mission. Now all of this is predicated upon intimacy with God. And not only does it require intimacy, it also facilitates intimacy. Intimacy with God is really the issue here. The phrase "walking with God" is used throughout the book of Genesis, and it always denotes ongoing relationship and intimacy. We know Noah walked with God,[1] as did Abraham[2] and Isaac.[3] Whenever that phrase is used, it's a metaphor for a real, meaningful relationship with God.

---

1. See Genesis 6:9.
2. See Genesis 17:1; 24:41; 48:15.
3. See Genesis 48:15.

Walking with God must be pleasing to God. Amos 3:3 says, "Do two walk together unless they have agreed to do so?" (*NIV*). Walking with another person suggests a mutual agreement—because if you're going to walk with somebody, you have to agree on a few things. In fact, it's impossible to walk with somebody unless you concur on these three things:

1. The place to which you are walking
2. The path upon which you are walking
3. The pace at which you are walking[4]

If we're going to walk with anybody, we must agree upon the place, the path and the pace.

Are We Headed to the Same Place?

To walk together, you must first agree upon the place or the destination. One of the "fun" things to do when you're married is to go shopping together. Any husband and wife that have ever headed out to the mall have discovered that the paths to the shoe store and to the electronics store are not the same. What happens? Conflict. At least for a moment there comes a realization that "We can't walk together!" We could separate, go to our own places and then rendezvous again later—and that would be fine in this context. But the goal of the Christian life is to walk *with* Jesus, not to separate and go our own way for a while.

Now as we seek to apply the Scriptures—which we must do—we have to ask ourselves: Are we heading to God's place? In our daily lives, are we moving in God's direction? Have we agreed with Him upon the final destination? Now of course, as Christians, we agree that we want to go to heaven. Great destination. That's where we want to be. That's a no-brainer. But what about in your daily life, in the small things, and

---

4. Adapted from R. Kent Hughes, *Preaching the Word: Hebrews*, vol. 2 (Wheaton, IL: Crossway Books, 1993), pp. 77-78.

in your goals for the day? Have you and the Lord agreed upon the place, the goal, the destination? If we're going to walk with God, we've got to be going to the same place—daily.

Glory Seekers

Understanding what is most important to God will help us to discover whether or not we have agreed on the destination as we walk with Him. What is most important to God is an important question for us to consider. If we really love someone, we are going to want to know what is most important to him or her. Because if we love that person, what is important to him or her becomes important to us! Do you love God? Then ponder this question: *What is the most important thing to God?* Here's the answer: *His glory.* God's glory is the single most important thing to Him. His glory is more important than you, the earth, and all of creation. In fact, all of creation declares His glory![5] God's glory is the most important thing.

When we think about glory, we get wrapped up in the idea of our own glory because we're glory seekers. This is part of our fallenness. We have difficulty understanding it because we are perverted. We are wrong in so much of our thinking. The fact that we seek our own glory is part of our distrust and mistrust of God. And when we seek our own glory, consciously or otherwise, it is always a sin against God. God is not one to share His glory. Though many of us do this in all sorts of ways, most of us realize deep down that seeking glory for ourselves is wrong.

Psalm 57:5 says, "Be exalted above the heavens, O God; let Your glory be above all the earth." It is not wrong for God to seek His own glory, and being made in the image of God, and redeemed by the cross, we are able to reflect a measure of that glory toward Him. But we need to be careful not to project our sinfulness toward God, because there is nothing about sin that glorifies Him. Think about it this way: God,

---

5. See Psalm 19:1.

being just, wise and altogether right, is concerned with the right things. And in the entire universe, there is nothing more right than the glory of God. And nothing more wrong than sin, which is totally void of God's glory.

For many years I shaped surfboards for a living. When I did well at it, it brought me a certain amount of recognition, praise and fame. Glory, you might say. Like anyone else, I loved the glory. And while making surfboards wasn't all glory—there were times when I failed—there was enough glory to give me a taste for it. So one of my primary motivations became glory. I was a glory seeker. Guess what I found? Glory is readily available. There are plenty of people who are happy to heap praise on someone with a little talent. That is abundantly evident in our idol-oriented society. But the Lord began to deal with me. He started to teach me that I did not exist to be praised by people, but rather to give praise to God.

So I did something very simple, yet very profound for me: I started to proclaim the glory of God on every surfboard I made. When I was done shaping it, I would write something on it for everyone to see. Whether they liked it or not didn't matter to me; I was doing it for God. Sometimes I would put a passage from Scripture on the board, or just write "Glory to God" or "Jesus is Lord" real big. It didn't change the world, but it began to change my heart. My job, the stuff I had been doing totally for myself, was slowly, board by board, day by day, becoming less about me and more about God. Eventually, I began to see that God and I were now walking together! We were headed in the same direction.

Kingdom Builders

The next step in walking with God is understanding that He wants to build His kingdom. Now this can be a difficult idea for us because in our fallenness we are kingdom builders—but for all the wrong reasons. It's *our* kingdom that we love to build. We build for *our* reputation.

We're just like those who built the tower of Babel. That drive to build our own kingdom is in each one of us. It needs to be redeemed by the cross of Christ and the Spirit of God. We need to be kingdom builders and kingdom seekers, but building and seeking first *His* kingdom.[6]

For years, I worked to build a surfboard kingdom, but then discovered the joy of participating in the building of God's kingdom. What I did with surfboards and the surf industry was part of that, but there came to be more too. I found myself going in to work well before dawn so I could finish at noon and spend the bulk of the day studying and teaching the Bible and discipling people. I made a conscious decision that I would put more time into His kingdom than into my own. Now, I had the liberty to set my own schedule because of the nature of my job. Not everyone can do that, but everyone can begin to ask the Lord, and themselves, *What can I do with the time and resources I have to be part of building the kingdom of God for the glory of God?* Once we earnestly start asking ourselves this, things will begin to change. Unfortunately, most Christians never even think about asking that question.

And so to align our lives with God's goals, to walk with God, we have to be concerned with building His kingdom, because that is another one of His priorities. After all, it was Jesus Himself who taught us to pray, "Thy kingdom come, Thy will be done on earth as it is in heaven."[7] So as Christians, we must ask ourselves, "How can I manifest God's kingdom around me, here and now? What about my workplace, with my co-workers? How can I bring a little bit of God's kingdom into my cubicle? How can I bring God's kingdom into my recreation? How can I manifest a little bit of God's kingdom, God's glory, God's purposes, the gospel of Christ, in my relationships? How can I seek first the kingdom of God in my finances?" If we want to truly walk with God, we need to ask ourselves questions like these and align our priorities with God's.

---

6. See Matthew 6:33.
7. Matthew 6:10, *KJV*.

So to walk with God, the Christian needs to be concerned with things that are consistent with the character of God and the plan of God. Seek to develop the character of God in your own life: mercy, grace, humility, love. Seek to do things that are consistent with the plan of God: carry out His justice and love in the world. Micah 6:8 makes it really clear:

He has told you, O man, what is good;
And what does the LORD require of you
But to do justice, to love kindness,
And to walk humbly with your God?

So we need to agree with God on the end goal, which is God's glory, God's kingdom, God's character, God's plan. And then we make decisions in our daily lives that are consistent with those goals, with that destination.

Get Swept Off Your Feet

Now how can we apply what happened to Enoch in our lives? It says in Hebrews 11:5 that Enoch was "taken up." It could also be translated he was "translated." Either way, the word used in the Greek, *metatithemi*, means that he was "carried across." It means to bear up, to remove, to change from one place to another. We have two ways in which we can apply Enoch to our lives: first, by thinking about the rapture. Enoch being taken directly to heaven without ever dying is a picture of the rapture of the Church, when Jesus will do the same thing for an entire generation. How miraculous will that be? I mean only Enoch and Elijah were ever taken up, but the Bible is explicit that a whole generation will be taken up and will not see death.

In 1 Corinthians 15, Paul speaks of the rapture of the Church. He says, beginning in verse 51, "Behold, I tell you a mystery; we will not all sleep [meaning die]." We will not all die. Do you know that Christianity is the only religion on earth that says there will be some people that will never die? In verses 52-53, Paul goes on to say that while we will not all die, we will all be changed "in a moment, in the twinkling of an eye, at the last trumpet; for the trumpet will sound, and the dead will be raised imperishable, and we will be changed. For this perishable must put on the imperishable, and this mortal must put on immortality."

This is speaking of the rapture of the Church. In 1 Thessalonians 4:17, Paul gives us more detail, describing that moment when Christ comes for His bride and we shall be "caught up together with them in the clouds to meet the Lord in the air, and so we shall always be with the Lord." Now, there is not only a catching up that happens at the rapture, but there is also a translation that happens. We are changed in the moment, in the twinkling of an eye, Paul says, because to live in the heavenly realm we need to replace this perishable body.

When we're truly living in the expectation that Jesus might come at any time, it changes the way that we live. We want to be on mission. We want to be involved in the work of the kingdom. We want to be running for God's glory, because we never know when He's going to come back, and we've got friends and family and community members that aren't saved yet. So having that expectation changes the way that I live. Suddenly I want to be about God's business, because I don't know when He's coming back again. And, just to be frank and very pragmatic, none of us want to be "that guy" who is living a life that isn't holy when Jesus returns, do we? When He comes—and we don't know when that is—I don't want to get caught with my hand in the cookie jar, so to speak. I want to be a man of character when He comes. I want to be about the business of God, consumed with the glory of God, running for the kingdom of God. In light of Jesus' coming, we should purify ourselves and make decisions differently about what we do and don't do—how we spend our time, money and other resources.[8]

8. See Romans 13:11-14; Ephesians 5:6-16; Titus 2:11-14; 2 Peter 3:9-14.

Living Up

The second way in which we can apply Enoch to our lives is by living up. In the rapture we'll be *going up*, but right now we need to be living up. In other words, transcending, living for the heavenlies, living above the darkness and drama of this world, and instead choosing to live according to the light and love and truth of Jesus Christ. This is reflected in Colossians 1:9-14. The apostle Paul, writing under the inspiration of the Holy Spirit, refers to the Colossians' love in the Spirit of which he had heard about:

> For this reason also, since the day we heard of it, we have not ceased to pray for you and to ask that you may be filled with the knowledge of His will in all spiritual wisdom and understanding, so that you will walk in a manner worthy of the Lord, to please Him in all respects, bearing fruit in every good work and increasing in the knowledge of God; strengthened with all power, according to His glorious might, for the attaining of all steadfastness and patience; joyously giving thanks to the Father, who has qualified us to share in the inheritance of the saints in Light. For He rescued us from the domain of darkness, and transferred us to the kingdom of His beloved Son, in whom we have redemption, the forgiveness of sins.

Now, in this passage Paul is speaking about living up to the truth of the cross of Jesus Christ and the relationship that we have with God. He is speaking about not allowing these things to be merely theoretical or philosophical or ethereal, but making them practical and letting them have a bearing on our daily lives. That is what the apostle Paul is praying for the Colossians. He wants their lives to be excellent in every way. He is reminding them that they have already been translated, or transferred, or taken up—in a sense like Enoch—since they had placed their faith in Christ.

Just like the Colossians, we Christians today need to think of ourselves as having had a change in address. In Colossians 1:13, Paul says that "He rescued us from the domain of darkness, and transferred us to the kingdom of His beloved Son." This is as real as the nose on your face. We have been delivered from the kingdom of darkness that is ruling in this world and we have been moved into the kingdom of Jesus Christ, who is the ruler of the entire universe. And this change, this move, is to have a practical bearing in the way that we live. Yes, we look forward to the day when we will be going up, but in the meantime, we need to be living up to the doctrines of God, the truth of God, the character of God and the standard of God.

We're to set our mind, our affections, our goals, our priorities on the things that are above—the reality of Jesus Christ and who He is. And then we're to live according to our new nature and not our old one. And in so doing, we're able to transcend, live up, live above the darkness, the drama, the evil and the heartbreak of this world, and live according to the light and love and truth of Jesus Christ.

The Power of Death Is Broken

In the story of Enoch, it says that he was "taken up so that he would not see death," meaning he didn't experience physical death. He never died. How stoked do you think he was? But there's something else to glean from this. While it is true that Enoch never physically died, there's another spiritual reality for Christians here. You see, Enoch being taken up without seeing death reveals to us that the power of death has been broken in the life of the Christian. Death comes because of sin. Romans 6:23 says, "The wages of sin is death." But the second part of that verse says, "But the free gift of God is eternal life in Christ Jesus." Jesus offers us eternal life, which nullifies and breaks the power of death because of the cross.

In John 11:25-26, Jesus said, "I am the resurrection and the life; he who believes in Me will live even if he dies, and everyone who lives and believes in Me will never die." So, in Jesus Christ we can have eternal life. But "eternal life" speaks not only of the length of life; it also speaks of the quality of life. It's not only a goal in the future; it is an actuality of the present. Eternal life is a quality of life by which we live according to the power of the Holy Spirit. We live according to the new life that we've been given in Christ Jesus. So the fact that Enoch did not experience death becomes metaphorical for us, a picture of the fact that we have eternal life, both the future hope of living forever with God *and* the immediate quality of that life that transcends the drama of the world. We have new life.

In Romans 6:4, Paul says, "Therefore we have been buried with [Christ] through baptism into death, so that as Christ was raised from the dead through the glory of the Father, so we too might walk in newness of life." That is what the Christian must endeavor to do. We need to walk in the new life that we've been given. We need to realize that we truly have been made brand new. As it says in 2 Corinthians 5:17, "Therefore if anyone is in Christ, he is a new creature; the old things passed away; behold, new things have come." All things have been made brand new. Therefore, to walk in newness of life means we have a new perspective. We have a new set of priorities. There is a new plan. There is a new power in which we live. There is a new place to which our gaze is fixed. There is new direction. There are new goals.

The Christian walks in newness of life. However, we cannot walk with God unless we've agreed on the place to which we are going, which is the glory of God, the kingdom of God, the character and the plan of God—all of which are made manifest in the life of the Christian through the salvation given to us through Jesus Christ. We are going up, but we also need to be living up, today.

Getting on the Same Path

Not only do we need to agree upon the *place*, but we also need to agree upon the *path* in order to walk with God. How can two walk together unless they're on the same path? Now it's interesting that you can be going to the same place with someone, but you can still take a different path. Walking with God means that we stay on the path of God. The reason Enoch's life is so profound is because he stayed on God's path. He stayed the course. What about your life? Right now—with the things that you're doing in your life—are you on God's path? Are you staying on God's course for you? Are you on track with what God has for your life? Are you living according to who Christ is and what He's done and what He's doing and is yet to do? Are you walking with God?

The difficulty in the Christian life is staying on course, isn't it? We usually get on course on Sunday. We hear the message and bam! Back on track. Beeline for heaven. But on Monday it's so easy to turn to the right or the left. Jesus tells us, however, that the Christian is to fix his or her hand to the plow and to not look back. Because when you plow, you want to plow a straight line. We're to stay on course with Jesus Christ. When Joshua was facing enormous challenges in taking the land of Canaan, God said to Joshua, "Only be strong and very courageous"—notice the phraseology—"be careful to do according to all the law, which Moses My servant commanded you; do not turn from it to the right or to the left, so that you may have success wherever you go."[9] Joshua was on the cusp of history. Prophetic history was unfolding. It was going to be tremendously difficult. He would live out the rest of his days in battle. But God told him to be careful. Be purposeful in obeying. Stay the course. Don't veer to the right or to the left. Stay the course and you will be successful.

Now that's a promise for you and me. Stay on God's path for your life and you'll be successful. Granted, you must rid yourself of the worldly concept of success. Get rid of it altogether. According to God's economy, you will be successful. The testimony of Enoch is that he pleased God. He was successful. That is success in life, pleasing God.

---

9. Joshua 1:7.

Moses told the nation of Israel to do this. In Deuteronomy 5:32, he said, "So you shall observe to do just as the LORD your God has commanded you; you shall not turn aside to the right or to the left." Proverbs 4:26-27 tells us the same thing:

Watch the path of your feet
And all your ways will be established.
Do not turn to the right nor to the left;
Turn your foot from evil.

Watch Your Step

Okay, here's the problem: We don't often watch the path of our feet. We go through life haphazardly, almost just letting it happen. But the Christian is to be on mission, and is to be purposeful for the glory of God and the kingdom of God according to the character of God and the plan of God. So it says in Scripture to watch the path of your feet, and very simply and poignantly, turn your feet from evil. We have the propensity of turning toward evil, don't we? But the Bible says to turn from evil. Don't go to it; flee from it.

Paul lived this way, and at the end of his life he was able to say, "I have fought the good fight, I have finished the course, I have kept the faith."[10] Paul knew that there was a course and that he needed to stick to it. He stuck with Jesus—even in the difficult times. And this is the protocol for the Christian: in difficult days, in tumultuous times, stick with Jesus. Stay the course, and cling to Him with every fiber of your being. Don't go to the right or the left. Walk *with* Him, to the same place on the same path.

How do we stay on God's path? Let's make it real simple. We have God's written Word, and we have God's prophetic voice, and we need to heed them both to stay on God's path. Psalm 119:105 in God's written Word says:

---

10. 2 Timothy 4:7.

Your word is a lamp to my feet
And a light to my path.

Begin to live according to the precepts that you find in Scripture and you will find yourself on the right path, with the way lit up before you. Take God's precepts one at a time as they intersect with your life. Adjust your life accordingly and you'll be on the right path. Then pay attention to the prophetic voice of God. God really does speak to people prophetically by His Spirit. He wants to speak into your life. Israel was told that they would have difficult days, but they were encouraged with these words in Isaiah 30:21:

Your ears will hear a word behind you, "This is the way, walk in it," whenever you turn to the right or to the left.

So whenever they were starting to veer, they would hear the prophetic voice of God saying "this way." Do you know that God wants to do that in your life? It says in Romans 8:14 that "all who are being led by the Spirit of God, these are sons of God." God wants to lead you daily in your relational choices, in your financial choices, in your choices of mission and vocation. He wants to lead you intimately and personally.

God Is Light

We are told in 1 John 1:5 that God is light: "This is the message we have heard from Him and announce to you, that God is Light, and in Him there is no darkness at all." And so, because the Bible tells us God is light, the Bible then tells us to walk in the light. Ephesians 5:8 says, "you were formerly darkness, but now you are Light in the Lord; walk as children of Light." So we walk in the light of God, the character of God, the truth of who Christ is, reflected in this world. Jesus said he who walks in the darkness doesn't know where he's going.[11] How do

---

11. See John 12:35.

we stay on course? God is light, so walk in the light! Shun the darkness of the world. Flee from evil. Have nothing to do with the deeds of darkness, even expose them. Ephesians says to walk in the light because God is light.

God Is Love

Scripture also tells us that God is love and that we are to walk in love. Twice in 1 John 4 it says that God is love. And in Ephesians 5:1-3, Paul says:

> Therefore be imitators of God, as beloved children; and walk in love, just as Christ also loved you and gave Himself up for us, an offering and a sacrifice to God as a fragrant aroma. But immorality or any impurity or greed must not even be named among you, as is proper among saints.

So, because God is love, the Christian is called to walk in love. We are to love in the same way that Christ loves us, giving the same grace, the same mercy toward people. Love covers a multitude of sins. As you walk in love, you release people from the bondage you're holding them in through your unforgiveness—and you release yourself from that bondage as well. Walking in love exhibits grace and mercy and forgiveness and is always reaching out. And because God is love, He's a God of mission. So when we walk in love, we walk on God's mission. And if the goal of God's mission is God's glory, then how do we exhibit the love of God in this world? We pursue His glory above all else.

God Is Truth

First John 5:20 tells us that God is truth. And then, in 2 John and 3 John, we're told to walk in the truth. Walking in the truth begins with *not* walking in lies. Shun the lies. Expose the lies. Get rid of the lies that you've been buying into—the lies that the enemy has sold you, the lies about identity, the lies about a lack of worth, the lies about self-entitlement, the lies about what you deserve. Free yourself from those lies. Walk in the truth, because the truth shall set you free.[12] God is truth; therefore, walk in truth. Don't believe the lies.

Walk at the Same Pace

To walk with God we first have to agree upon the *place*, then we have to agree upon the *path*, and finally, we have to agree upon the *pace*. If we're going to walk *with* Him, we have to travel at the same pace. You see, Enoch had a life of faith because he stayed in step with God. This is a big deal in the Christian life—it's essential. Galatians 5:25 urges us to "keep in step with the Spirit" (*NIV*), meaning we are not to get ahead of God in our life and, at the same time, not lag behind. It's really easy for us to get ahead of God. You know why? Trip out on this: Because God is outside of time and space—and has always been—He knows the beginning from the end. He already knows what's going to happen. He's not bound by the constraints of the time/space continuum like we are. Therefore, God is never in a hurry. We, on the other hand, are always in a hurry. That makes it hard for us to walk at the same pace.

In the Christian life we are not often struggling to keep up with God. It's more often us trying to slow down and chill. We struggle to be still and know that He is God,[13] just to stick with Him and not get ahead of Him. That's where we err—when we get ahead of God. And we have such a proclivity to do so. For example, we get ahead of God too easily in our finances, don't we? It has become a real problem for a lot of Americans—and a lot of American Christians. Getting ahead of God in our finances results in all sorts of bondage and problems that we would avoid just by walking at God's pace in this area.

---

12. See John 8:32.
13. See Psalm 46:10.

We often get ahead of God in our relationships as well. I've seen this happen more times than I've ever wanted to. I've seen a young lady choose the wrong guy, because in her loneliness she refused to wait for God. She demanded that this be the one. And I've seen the utter destruction that decision brings—destruction in lives for generations. Walk at God's pace in your relationships.

Walking with Consistency

Don't get ahead of God. At the same time, don't lag behind. It's real simple. Keep in step with the Spirit. It takes daily, purposeful action—the conscious, intentional seeking of God—to stay in step with His Spirit in your life and for your life. This requires consistency. Uh-oh. We're not real good at consistency, are we? So many of us are the up-and-down, start-and-stop, run-fast-and-poop-out type. But the Christian life is one of discipline. We're called *disciples* of Jesus Christ. That word "disciple" shares its etymology with the word "discipline." The Christian must have discipline. To walk with God implies and requires consistency, diligence, perseverance and dedication.

Walking with Dedication

Are you at the point in your life that God is calling you to change direction and walk with Him? You may need to do an about-face. Enoch did. It says in Genesis 5:21 that he lived 65 years for himself and then he fathered Methuselah. And the next verse says, "Then Enoch walked with God for 300 years." Even after 65 years of self-absorbed living, it wasn't too late. He did an about-face. He repented. He said, "No more of this. I'm going to walk with God." And he walked so close to God that he lived out the meaning of his name, which is "dedicated."

If your life right now is all about *you*, *your* glory, *your* kingdom, *your* purposes and *your* plans, then you are headed in the wrong direction. It's all about God's glory, God's kingdom, God's purposes and

God's plan. So to walk with God, we need to agree with Him on the place, on the path and on the pace. It's going to require consistency, dedication and faith.

5

FAITH WORKING

Noah

By faith Noah, being warned by God about things not yet seen, in reverence prepared an ark for the salvation of his household, by which he condemned the world, and became an heir of the righteousness which is according to faith.

HEBREWS 11:7

IN HEBREWS 11:7, NOAH IS HELD UP AS A MODEL OF MEANINGFUL FAITH FOR US.

He is our example of faith working. I know you know the story of Noah. But have you ever stopped to consider the scale of what Noah actually did? Noah did a really big job. I don't know if you know how big the ark was, but this was a big job for some cat to do. It had to be done right, with the right attitude and the right approach. And Noah was just the man for the job. So while Abel exemplified faith worshiping God, and Enoch exemplified faith walking with God, Noah exemplifies faith working for God. And this is the order of things as ordained by God.

Our God is a God of order, and He orders things as He wishes. In creation, there's a certain order that speaks of a Creator. In Scripture, there's a certain order that speaks of a God who is concerned with the priority of things and instructs us on how to prioritize our lives. It starts with authentic and sincere worship of God, which yields a life of walking with God, which then will produce fruitful work for God. A.W. Tozer says that when we catch the true life of worship, then the work that flows out of it will have eternity in it.[1]

The truth is that ministry should flow from intimacy. Because of the fallen nature of man and our own proclivity toward rebellion—even after having been born again—we know how to order our lives, but we have a tendency to change that order or, even worse, to skip steps altogether. We realize from Hebrews 11 that Enoch's *walk* of faith had to come before Noah's *work* of faith. And Abel's *worship* in faith had to precede both of them. Here's the order of life: the worship of Christ, the walk with Christ, *and then* working for Christ. That's the order of things. Worship God, then walk with God, and then work for God. And as we strive to live the life of faith, we're not to reverse that order.

---

1. A. W. Tozer, *Worship: The Missing Jewel in the Evangelical Church* (Camp Hill, PA: Christian Publications, 1996); *Gems from Tozer* (Camp Hill, PA: Christian Publications, 1979), p. 15.

Working for vs. Being with Him

We often make the mistake of giving priority to working for God *over* worshiping God and walking with Him. This can be a huge failure for us individually as Christians and corporately as the Church. I've noticed a tendency toward this in my own life. As a pastor of a growing church, a pastor to other pastors, and a pastor to church planters, I have a lot of responsibilities—a lot of stuff that God has called me to do. And with all the demands, I find myself becoming all about the *doing* when God is all about the *being*. For me it can easily become just about the ministry, and the ministry can become the goal. We all know that ministry is not the goal. The glory of Jesus Christ is the goal. But many of us are people that like to just "git'r done." We can be like that. At least I know *I'm* like that. That's just my personality. To avoid this mentality, I have to reprioritize frequently—daily, in fact. I have to slow down and tell myself, "It's not about what I'm doing for God; it's about being with God. It's not about working for Him; it's about worshiping Him." I need to slow down to stop and think about that daily.

The story of Jesus' interaction with Martha and Mary in Luke 10 brings this home for me. First we see Martha busy with all this stuff, working for and serving the Lord. It was a noble thing for sure. Jesus was in her house and Martha said, "I want to make Him a meal." That's not a bad thing. So while Martha made Jesus a meal, her sister Mary sat around at Jesus' feet, listening to Him speak. Martha got all bummed out! We—and I say "we" because I'm this way—often get all bummed out when someone's not doing enough. So Martha said, "Lord! Tell Mary to help me out here!" Jesus responded, "Martha, Martha . . . you are worried and upset about many things, but only one thing is needed. Mary has chosen what is better, and it will not be taken away from her."[2]

All Mary did was sit at the Lord's feet, listening to His word. That bugged Martha the worker, but it pleased the Lord Jesus Christ. He

---

2. Luke 10:41-42, *NIV.*

is the only One we need to please. We don't live to please pastors; we don't live to please churches; we don't live to please organizations. We don't live to please other people; we don't even live to please ourselves. We live to please Jesus Christ! Mary prioritized just being with Jesus, and poured the alabaster vial of perfume out onto His feet in worship. As a result, Jesus said Mary would be remembered wherever the gospel went forth.[3] He didn't say that about Abraham, though he's the father of faith. He didn't say that about anybody else in all of Scripture. He didn't even say it about good old Noah. Only about Mary, and all she did was give priority to the act of worship.

God Wants You

Before we can fully grasp how we are to work for Christ, we must first understand the basis on which we are invited into God's work. Scripture makes it clear that God is at work; He is a missionary God, and He is on a mission in the world around you—at your workplace, in your family, amongst your friends. It's not the church's mission; it is not our mission; it is His mission. God is on a mission and He invites us to participate.

First, it is essential to understand that God does not *need* you. He doesn't need your or my help to accomplish His mission. God is all-sufficient. He existed a long time before you ever did, and He was just fine without you. Just like your parents. Remember when you were growing up and you got to that arrogant adolescent stage when you thought your parents were idiots? Remember that? It seemed like that phase lasted so long for me. I'm sorry, Mom and Dad. Forgive me. But you remember that stage when you're telling your parents, "Duh! What are you doing? Don't you understand?" I remember my dad looking at me and saying, "Britt, somehow I survived a long time before you were ever born." You know, he didn't need me in that sense.

---

3. See Mark 14:3-9.

He was okay before I came along. But he loves me. In the same way, God doesn't need you. He really doesn't need you, but He loves you.

The idea that God doesn't need us when it comes to His work should be incredibly freeing to us! You know why? Because in most cases we're already overwhelmed by the needs of others. We are all surrounded by people who need us—at work and at home. My coworkers need me. My daughter needs me. My son needs me. My wife needs me. My friends need me. And now God needs me too? What a relief to realize that He doesn't. God will accomplish His work—with or without you. But He loves you, and because He does, He invites you to participate. Isn't it true that love, by nature, is invitational? Love reaches out and includes. That's what love does. God loves you, so He wants to include you in His passions and in His mission. That's why He invites you in. For example, I love my son, so I try to include him in the things that I do. I'm into dirt biking, so I got him a little mini dirt bike. I love surfing, so he's got a little surfboard. I love playing guitar and so I got him a little guitar! When we love someone, we want to include them in our passions, and involve them in the things we are doing.

That is why we work for God. Not because He needs us to, but because He wants us to—He wants to be with us. But you see, the fundamental failure is that we try to work for God before marinating in the love of God. Because the mission and the invitation and the great commission flow out of that love relationship, if we get the priority wrong, it just doesn't work right. Worship God and walk with God so that you might experience the fullness of His love—and love Him back. And *then* work will flow out of that. You know, if you just worship God and walk with God long enough, you'll get involved in God's work. Don't even worry about it. Nobody's going to have to pressure or coerce you. Your church and your pastors aren't going to have to put a heavy weight on you. If you're a worshiper, you'll become a worker. It will just happen naturally. But if you're a worker that's not worshiping, you had better get right. Because if you don't, it could just shipwreck your life.

Noah Knew How to Work for God

Noah exemplifies faith working in the right way and the right order. Genesis 6:5-14 gives us a good picture of Noah's situation and the work he had to do:

> Then the LORD saw that the wickedness of man was great on the earth, and that every intent of the thoughts of his heart was only evil continually.
>
> The LORD was sorry that He had made man on the earth, and He was grieved in His heart.
>
> The LORD said, "I will blot out man whom I have created from the face of the land, from man to animals to creeping things and to birds of the sky; for I am sorry that I have made them."
>
> But Noah found favor in the eyes of the LORD.
>
> These are the records of the generations of Noah. Noah was a righteous man, blameless in his time; Noah walked with God.
>
> Noah became the father of three sons: Shem, Ham, and Japheth.
>
> Now the earth was corrupt in the sight of God, and the earth was filled with violence.
>
> God looked on the earth, and behold, it was corrupt; for all flesh had corrupted their way upon the earth.
>
> Then God said to Noah, "The end of all flesh has come before Me; for the earth is filled with violence because of them; and behold, I am about to destroy them with the earth. Make for yourself an ark of gopher wood."

Three essential actions of the life of faith can be seen in Noah: *believe, adjust* and *build*. First he *believed* what God said about the future. Second, he *adjusted* his life accordingly. And third, he *built* the ark faithfully.

Before unpacking these concepts, I want to highlight Hebrews 11:7, where there were three outcomes to those three actions. First, Noah's family was saved. Second, the wicked were proven wrong. And third, Noah was considered righteous. So Noah's life of faith accomplished those three very important things. Don't let them be abstract ideas. His family was saved—think about your own husband or wife and your kids in this world. The wicked were proven wrong—think about the voices today that are dissenting, attacking and trying to detract from the authority of the Bible and the person of Jesus Christ. Noah was considered righteous—think about your standing before God. Notice that Noah was considered righteous because of faith, not because of work.

Noah Believed

With reverence and obedience Noah took God at His Word. If you think about it, it would have been very easy for Noah to think that God's Word was foolishness. Yet he believed it. More importantly, he staked everything on it. Noah had a lot less evidence for believing God—and a lot more opposition—than we have today. Today, we have the Church, a remnant of believers in the world. But back in the day, there wasn't *anybody* for God but Noah. Everybody else was against God. Yet Noah believed.

In the last chapter, we looked at place, path and pace. Like Enoch, Noah was going to God's place on God's path at God's pace. In Genesis 6:8-9 we read, "Noah found favor in the eyes of the Lord . . . Noah was a righteous man, blameless in his time; Noah walked with God." Noah walked with God, and that profoundly affected his life. His life became concentrated and purposeful for God's plan—because he chose to believe.

Now that choice is before every one of us—whether or not you're going to believe God and act on that belief. By believing God, Noah avoided disaster, and not only for himself, but also for his family. Noah did not pick and choose what he would believe and what he would obey. He believed and obeyed *exactly* as the Lord said, as it says later on in the sixth and seventh chapters of Genesis.[4] By believing and obeying, Noah avoided disaster in his life and in the lives of his whole family. As a father and as a husband, I would have been concerned, too. I want the wellbeing of my family, and I begin to understand that the wellbeing of my family is to some degree dependent on my obedience as a man of God. It's dependent on my faith and my choice to believe God and act upon that belief. Sin is the opposite of belief and obedience. Although I would love it if my sin was totally isolated and never affected anybody else, the reality is that my sin affects my wife, my kids and the people that I pastor. And their sin affects me. That's just the way God designed it to be. Sin doesn't happen in a vacuum.

So through Noah's careful obedience—which resulted from his authentic faith—he saved himself and his family from disaster. God warned him and he heeded the warning. Now, we are warned all the time. Psalm 19:11 says that by the Scriptures a servant of God is warned, and warnings come to us in a lot of ways. Warnings come to us through the Bible, through God's prophetic voice, through the Church and through our conscience (which is a gift from God). Warnings come to us through advice and rebuke from godly people. Warnings might come to us through a sermon or a book. And warnings can even come to us through our circumstances. Whichever way they come, the question really is, *What will we do with those warnings when we receive them?* If we neglect them, we put ourselves and our families in danger. God told Joshua in Joshua 1:7:

> Only be strong and very courageous; be careful to do according to all the law which Moses My servant commanded you; do not turn from it to the right or to the left, so that you may have success wherever you go.

---

4. See Genesis 6:22; 7:5.

We have all these warnings from God because He cares. When my family goes on walks in our neighborhood, my little Daisy Love rides her tiny bike. She's on training wheels, and she's just nuts on that bike. She loves to speed ahead and just swerve around. We live on a fairly busy street, so I'm always saying, "Daisy, there's a car coming!" "Daisy there's a car up there!" "Daisy, they can't see you up there!" "Daisy, you're going around the corner. Slow down!" "Daisy, pull over to the side!" As a father who radically loves her, I am always warning her. If she ignores these warnings, it puts her life in danger. That's a living parable of the relationship between you and God. He is your Father who radically and desperately loves you, who is concerned with all your comings and your goings.[5] And when you ignore Him, you put yourself and your family in danger.

God's warnings are given out of His love for us. And when we believe them, our sincere belief will always bring life adjustment. If Daisy believes me when I warn her that a car is coming, she is going to adjust her course and pull over to the side. She's going to adjust her speed and slow down and stop. Sincere belief will bring life adjustment. Adjustments are those things we do to make our lives more in harmony with and more aligned with God's heart and God's will. Adjustments are acts of obedience, and obedience and faith are bound up together. It was faith that caused Noah to obey, and moved him to action. Faith moves us to action. If you trust God, you will obey God. What you *do* is what you truly *believe*. Noah made evident what he believed by what he did. Don't *tell* me what you believe; *show* me what you believe—by your actions. That's what the Bible says in James 2:14-20. You know that old saying, "Actions speak louder than words"? It's true. And nowhere is this more true than in the realm of Christianity.

Noah Rearranged His World

There's no doubt that Noah had to radically rearrange his life to do what God was calling him to do. God called him to build a boat, and according

---

5. See Psalm 139:1-3.

to Genesis 6:3, it would be 120 years that he would be building that boat—120 years of his life! That required a few adjustments! Some little changes in the schedule. You know, he probably got out his day planner and said, "Oh, boy, I am just slammed. I mean, whew. Let's see . . . how about 80 years from now? Oh, Lord, I'm totally booked. I mean I could pencil You in, in like 90 years. How would that work for You?" Well, that doesn't work with God. Noah had to make some adjustments right then and there to align himself with God's will and God's purpose. And I imagine that he probably didn't always feel like it. There were probably days that Noah woke up and looked at the pile of gopher wood and just said, "Oy vey! Not again. Really? Building again?! I mean this thing is taking forever!" The boat was 450 feet long, you understand. Seventy-five feet wide. Forty-five feet high. That is a big old boat, all built without power tools! Noah was committed to the task for 120 years. To commit to that task, he had to make some adjustments in his life.

Adding More Hours to My Day

In my early twenties I really fell in love with Jesus Christ and had to make some major adjustments. I became a true worshiper and really started to walk with Jesus. He opened my eyes to the mission field around me. I realized the kids I surfed with every day at Tar Pits, my local beach, knew nothing about Jesus. I sensed I was being invited into the work of God. I had never felt this before, but now that I was a worshiper and walking with God, I knew that He wanted me to begin working for Him as well, telling these kids about Jesus. If you grew up with me, you'd know that I was not a likely candidate for the job.

So I started telling these kids about Jesus and invited them over to my parents' house for a Bible study and some of them got saved. The Bible study grew and it turned into a college ministry at a church in Santa Barbara that grew to several hundred people. During this time I also worked in the family business making surfboards. I shaped surfboards, coached our amateur team, recruited people for the team, and did all of the marketing and advertising for the company. So I had an incredibly full plate at Channel Islands Surfboards. Meanwhile, the little ministry the Lord had given me was really growing. Hundreds of people were now involved. That meant that not only was I teaching, but I was also now getting invitations to go all around the world to teach the Bible, which required that I study a lot. I was also discipling quite a bit. Lots of young men needed me to disciple them. This required a lot of time spent mentoring and counseling during camps and trips. All good stuff, but a tremendous demand upon my time. Without a doubt I knew God had called me into these missions, but it seemed like 20 hours in a day were just not enough.

That's when I knew I had to adjust my life. I decided I would get up at 4 A.M. every morning to spend time with the Lord, to prepare my heart to do the work I was doing with Him and for Him. I'd sit in my chair and drink some tea or some coffee, read the Bible, worship God and just spend time with Him. I'd be done before the sun came up, and then I could go to the family business and shape surfboards and I'd be done by noon. And then I was out of there to disciple, to minister, to study, to teach, to lead and to do all the other things that God had called me to do. But it took a radical adjustment in my life. Basically, I gave up sleeping! That worked for me. It doesn't work for everybody.

Adjusting = Giving Something Up

I had to make adjustments for me to be obedient. I gave up things like going on snowboarding trips and surf trips and going to surf contests and doing all these other fun things. I gave up hanging out for hours playing guitar with my friends—one of my favorite things to do. I just didn't have time anymore. So I laid those things aside to be obedient to what God had called me to do. What I found is that God is a giver, not a taker. For everything that I surrendered to Him, He blessed me with far more than I could have ever imagined. That's just how God is.

99

Most Americans acknowledge that they need to make major life changes, according to a recent poll done by The Barna Group. Most adults (55 percent) reject the statement "you would not change anything significant about your life."[6] People *want to* adjust, to make the changes necessary to accomplish and attain the things in life that they want. However, many people are not willing to *actually do* what it takes to adjust. They just don't want to. Maybe they have an aversion to change. I think we all do to some degree. Or maybe they have grown accustomed to comfort, rest, recreation and relaxation. Very seldom do people trust God enough to surrender those things and believe that they'll actually be satisfied in Christ. And that's too bad, because He is faithful to meet the desires of our heart when we put our trust, our faith, in Him and adjust our lives. As Psalm 37:4 tells us, "Delight yourself in the Lord; and He will give you the desires of your heart."

I know that I'm way more stoked on Jesus than I ever was on snowboarding. I'm way more satisfied in Jesus Christ than I ever was in Fiji, Hawaii or wherever I surfed. I'm far more satisfied in Christ. I'm sure Noah radically rearranged his life to do what God called him to do. We're not told about the life Noah had before the ark, but we can assume he had a life. He probably did a few things before God said, "Oh, Noah, by the way, would you build a 450-foot boat for the next 120 years?" He had to adjust. He did so with the faith—sincere faith—that will always allow you to make adjustments so that you can build for God's purposes.

Building with God

Building is what we do when we are convinced that God's will, glory, and kingdom are most important. When we believe, we adjust and begin to build for the cause of God's glory and kingdom and according

---

6. "American Spirituality Gives Way to Simplicity and the Desire to Make a Difference," The Barna Group, October 27, 2008. http://www.barna.org/barna-update/article/12-faithspirituality/19-american-spirituality-gives-way-to-simplicity-and-the-desire-to-make-a-difference.

to His will. So if you want to live a life of faith, you need to ask yourself what you believe God has said or is doing and then how you should adjust. What does God want to do in your marriage? What does God want to do with your kids? What does God want to do in your workplace or with your business? What is God doing in your church? In your community? In the nations? How do you need to adjust in each, or all, of these areas? What you believe God is doing and has said about the future will determine how you should adjust and how you can build for His purposes.

What keeps you from adjusting? What is it that you're holding on to so tightly? God is not a life wrecker. He's not a joy robber. He really does want you to live joyously. When I radically adjusted my life, I got satisfaction, fulfillment, joy and wonder in return. Noah radically adjusted his life, and it saved him, his family and the entire human race! I don't understand why people think that God is out to wreck our lives. They think, *If I adjust my life, He's going to send me in the deepest, darkest jungle and people are gonna eat me!* It's totally possible. But if that happens, believe it or not, you'll be totally stoked! That's the way God is. You won't find a single missionary that spent his life in the jungle among cannibals that says, "Well, that stunk." None of them will say that. In all of their assessments, it was a life well spent. But there are not a lot of people who truly believe that.

Culture, Call and Task

Noah's work of faith was because he believed, adjusted and then built. Why did that require faith? For three reasons: *culture, call* and *task*. Noah's work required faith because of the culture he lived in, because of the call he received and because of the task he took on. Here's what we know about Noah's culture. It was wicked—exceedingly wicked. Genesis 6:5 and 11 tell us that. It required faith for Noah to obey in that culture, because no one held his hand. He had no support group, no church, no home group, or even anyone cheering him on, holding him accountable or showing him how. There was no prayer ministry for him, no one helping him, no one leading him and nobody following him either. So it really took faith—faith that many of us have never experienced or even seen.

Don't you think people mocked him? He didn't care. Although he lived in the region of Mesopotamia between the Euphrates and the Tigris Rivers, hundred of miles from an ocean, Noah still built the ark without ever seeing a boat before. In fact, nobody had ever seen a boat. This was the first boat. But there he was, building a 450-foot boat for 120 years. I imagine in the first year he was pretty bold. Just kicking butt. He must have been up there building that boat, and people would come along and say, "Noah! What are you doing?" And he would say, "Oh, I'm building a boat, because God says judgment is coming. A flood is coming! And you're wicked and you're perverse and you need to repent! Pursue the glory of God, you scoundrel vermin!"

And Noah just kept building the boat. Maybe ten years into it, people were saying, "Noah, come on, dude, what are you doing?" And Noah would say, "I'm building a boat and you ought to repent because pretty soon this flood is coming, so you better get right!" Can you imagine 90 years into it? "Hey, Noah! What are you doing?" "Oh, I don't know. I'm not exactly sure . . ." But that's not what we hear about Noah. Second Peter 2:5 tells us that Noah was a preacher of righteousness, and because it says it without qualification, we can assume he was *the whole time*. Noah stayed on task in the midst of a wicked and perverse generation for 120 years. That took great faith.

Noah's culture was wicked, but his *call* was unprecedented. Noah was hundreds of miles from the ocean and there had never been a flood. But he believed God. That's faith. Remember Hebrews 11:1? It's being sure of things we hope for and knowing that something is real even if we don't see it. Noah simply believed the Lord. And his righteousness consisted of the fact that he took God at His Word, even though his call was unprecedented. They had no context for it! When other men broke God's commandments, Noah kept them. When other men were deaf to God's warnings, Noah listened. When other men laughed at God, Noah revered Him. When other men disregarded God, Noah saw Him as the Supreme Reality in the world.

Why Noah Is Relevant Today

Today, we live in a cultural context more similar to Noah's than we may think. Like Noah, we live in the midst of extreme wickedness and coming judgment. In Matthew 24:37-39, Jesus used the story of Noah to speak about His coming:

> When the Son of Man returns, it will be like it was in Noah's day. In those days before the flood, the people were enjoying banquets and parties and weddings right up to the time Noah entered his boat. People didn't realize what was going to happen until the flood came and swept them all away. That is the way it will be when the Son of Man comes (*NLT*).

Not only do we live in a culture more similar to Noah's than we think, but we also have a call more similar to Noah's than we think. Hebrews 11:7 says, "By faith Noah, being warned by God about things not yet seen, in reverence prepared the ark for salvation of his household." That was his call. He prepared. That word "prepare" in the Greek means to furnish, to adorn fully, to get ready. We are told again and again in the New Testament to get ready for the coming of the Lord and to be involved in the work of God's kingdom because He's coming very soon. We are told to be involved in the work of evangelism and to be about our Father's business, preparing for His return. Our call is just like Noah's.

Now today, we don't need to prepare an ark. For us, Christ is the ark. Noah's ark was a prophetic picture, a foreshadowing of Jesus Christ. Christ alone is the one that saves us from the judgment. We *are* called to get people into the ark. In partnership with God, we're called to invite people in. In Noah's day, his building of the ark was a sermon in itself. Just the act of obeying God was a testimony to the wicked world. He had a life that was changed and purposeful. And even though nobody understood, Noah's life was a sermon. Like Noah, we preach the gospel not just with our words but also with our actions. Actions speak louder than words. As Saint Francis of Assisi said, "Preach the gospel at all times—if necessary, use words."

Noah believed God and he acted on that belief, even though what he believed would not arrive for 120 years! Now I believe we're a lot closer to the coming of the Lord than 120 years. Because I believe it, I'm going to order my life accordingly. Jesus said that if you don't think He's coming back soon—if you have an attitude and a mindset that says, "Oh, pff! Tsh!!! He's not comin' for a long time"—you're in real trouble!

Listen to what Jesus said in Matthew 24:44-51:

For this reason you also must be ready; for the Son of Man is coming at an hour when you do not think He will. Who then is the faithful and sensible slave whom his master put in charge of his household to give them their food at the proper time? Blessed is that slave whom his master finds so doing when he comes. Truly I say to you that he will put him in charge of all his possessions. But if that evil slave says in his heart, "My master is not coming for a long time," and begins to beat his fellow slaves and eat and drink with drunkards; the master of that slave will come on a day when he does not expect him and at an hour which he does not know, and will cut him in pieces and assign him a place with the hypocrites; in that place there will be weeping and gnashing of teeth.

I'm not exactly sure what that means, but it doesn't sound good. Therefore, because Jesus Christ said He's coming again, we need to make adjustments to our lives so we can build for God's glory, like

Noah did. The culture and the call that we have in common with Noah beckon us to build for God.

And finally, we have a task more similar to Noah's than we think. While Noah confronted culture with his obedience, we're called to confront culture with Christ. We're not called to acquiesce to culture. We're not called to disengage from it either. Christians are not to be isolationists. We're called to engage and confront culture with the reality of Jesus Christ and the gospel. It's essentially the same task that Noah had. Hebrews 11:7 tells us that Noah did it with reverence. And that word "reverence" means to be thoughtful, cautious and circumspect—to be moved or impressed with natural, healthy fear. You see, Noah had a reverential fear of God that moved him to action. But today, there's a disconnect in how the Church views God. There's no fear of God anymore. We lack reverence for Him, because we have re-made Him in our own image. Jesus Christ has become our Bro. Our Homie. Our Friend. Our Problem-Solver. The Big Guy in the sky. That's not who He is. He's the eternal, everlasting God of the universe who is holy and righteous and demands our worship and deserves our worship. He is the One for whose glory we ought to live.

If you find you're lacking in reverence, maybe you need to return to that place of worshiping. The more you worship God, the more you realize how holy and awesome He is. Or maybe you need to focus on your walk with God, on just being with God. The more you walk with God, the more you realize how awesome He is—and how cheesy you are! And that gets us on task real quick. We start to say, "Wow, the world's not about me, is it? Gosh! For a minute there I really thought it was."

Just Do It

To borrow a popular line, it's not about you. It's not about your stuff and your wants. God wants to bless you, but first you need to determine to go to God's place on God's path at God's pace. You need to believe and adjust and build. Like Noah, we live in a wicked culture. Also like

Noah, we have a profound call and a big task. We must commit ourselves to a life of faith, and do these things according to our belief that God will judge the world. To save us from eternal damnation and because of His love for us, He has provided a way for eternal life in heaven. Therefore we preach the gospel, in our family, with our kids, with our friends, at the workplace. Some of us aren't very gifted in speaking it. Maybe your gift is living it. That's awesome. We say it and we live it. But we do it.

In 1 Corinthians 15:58, Paul tells us, "Therefore, my beloved brethren, be steadfast, immovable, always abounding in the work of the Lord, knowing that your toil is not in vain in the Lord." I don't want to get to the end of my life and realize that everything was toil and vanity. I want to know the things I'm doing right now are not in vain. I want to know that I'm abounding in the work of the Lord. This is the call on your life just as it was for Noah: to be obedient and faithful to the task of living and proclaiming the gospel. That is all we are asked to do. The rest is up to God.

6

FAITH WILLING

Abraham

*By faith Abraham, when he was called,
obeyed by going out to a place which he
was to receive for an inheritance; and he
went out, not knowing where he was going.*

HEBREWS 11:8

WHEN IT COMES TO BIBLICAL FAITH,

Abraham is the preeminent figure. He's a major player in the Hall of Faith, and best known as "the father of faith." His story begins in Genesis 12:1-8:

> Now the LORD said to Abram, "Go forth from your country, and from your relatives and from your father's house, to the land which I will show you; and I will make you a great nation, and I will bless you, and make your name great; and so you shall be a blessing; and I will bless those who bless you, and the one who curses you I will curse and in you all the families of the earth will be blessed."
>
> So Abram went forth as the LORD had spoken to him; and Lot went with him. Now Abram was seventy-five years old when he departed from Haran. Abram took Sarai his wife and Lot his nephew, and all their possessions which they had accumulated, and the persons which they had acquired in Haran, and they set out for the land of Canaan; thus they came to the land of Canaan.
>
> Abram passed through the land as far as the site of Shechem, to the oak of Moreh. Now the Canaanite was then in the land. The LORD appeared to Abram and said, "To your descendants I will give this land." So he built an altar there to the LORD who had appeared to him. Then he proceeded from there to the mountain on the east of Bethel, and pitched his tent, with Bethel on the west and Ai on the east; and there he built an altar to the LORD and called upon the name of the LORD.

When we look at Abraham, we see a life of faith that is *willing*. Abel was faith worshiping. Enoch pictured faith walking. Noah taught us about faith working, and Abraham exemplifies a faith that is willing to respond to God. When God spoke to Abraham, he listened. When God promised, he trusted. When God commanded, he obeyed. We learn four things about Abraham: he had the willingness to go, forego, worship and witness.

Willing to Go

Abraham's willingness to go is as important as his going *without knowing where*. Now that's a big deal. I believe there's a very clear reason why. Look at Genesis 12. The first three verses are one long sentence, and God says something five different times in that one sentence. God says the words "I will" five times there. Genesis 12:1-3 is the famous Abrahamic covenant—the promise that God made to Abraham. Now the thrust of this covenant is not on the *"Would you, Abraham,"* but rather on the *"I will"* of God. The weight is not on what Abraham is being asked to do, but what God promises to do. And because God's Word came to Abraham as *"Go and I will do this for you,"* Abraham was willing to go.

This should be true in our lives. We should have a faith that is willing because God first said, "I will." Because of what the Bible says, we are willing to respond with faith and obedience. Living on this side of the cross, we have a faith that is willing because Jesus Christ was willing, because Jesus says, "I have." *"Tetelestai!"* He said on the cross, "I have done it; it is finished!" The price for our sins was paid in full. We respond in gratitude for what the Lord has done.

That's what's going on with Abraham. Five times God said to him, "I will accomplish these things." So when God told Abraham to go, Abraham didn't have to know *where*; he simply knew that God *would*, and so he went. That's trust. That's faith. The vagueness of God's directive to Abraham made it a real decision of faith. God simply said, "Go."

Now, we don't know all the particulars of what happened when Abraham "went forth." I know that if God just said "go" to me, I would want a few more details about where. When Jesus called the disciples, He simply walked up to them and said, "Follow Me." He didn't give any details. I mean, what did Abraham and Sarah and Lot do when they walked out the front door? How did they know? What was the plan? Go straight for 400 miles, veer left at those oaks, and then it's the first valley on your right?

We just don't have the details. We don't know exactly *how* the Spirit of God led them, but we do know that the Spirit of God led them. We know we have the same promise. Romans 8:14 says, "For all who are being led by the Spirit of God, these are sons of God." God is the God of details so that we don't have to be caught up in and worried about them. But we have this real tendency to get caught up in the details. We all want more details from the story of Abraham. When he walked out his door, how did he know whether to go right or left? What did he do?

The Spirit of God led Abraham. He wasn't told about Canaan until after he "went forth." That's cool, because the uncertainty of the command forced Abraham to rely simply upon God's Word. Calvin called this the *verbum nudum*: the "naked Word of God" in Latin. It was beyond what Abraham could see. It was beyond understanding; it was beyond what he was feeling. But we get so caught up in our feelings, don't we? We are always asking, "How do you *feel* about it? Oh, I'm not sure how I *feel* about it. I'm not *feeling* very good." Or, "I have a weird *feeling*. Oh, it doesn't *feel* right." It's just part of our everyday language. It's our grammar. But the *verbum nudum*, the naked Word of God, supersedes how you feel.

The *verbum nudum* also supersedes what you see. We love the seen. We love the tangible and the visual and the visceral. We love that. "If I could just get my hands on it," we say. "If You would just lay the plan out for me in black and white, Lord. If You would just put it up on a signpost." I mean if the writing was on the wall like that whole "MENE, MENE, TEKEL, UPHARSIN" thing in Daniel, then I would go.[1] But all Abraham had was the bare, naked Word of God and that really required faith. He didn't know the end game necessarily. I mean he knew that God said He would make a great nation of him, but at age 75, poor Abe didn't have any kids yet! He didn't know all the details that would get him from here to there. He just knew God would do what He said He would.

---

1. See Daniel 5.

When God Says Go

In 2003, my wife and I were up at my parent's little family cabin overlooking a lake in Idaho, just enjoying life and having a good time. We just had one child, a couple of years old at the time, and we enjoyed a great life. I worked at the family surfboard business and was also doing the college ministry at a church in Santa Barbara. I could've kept this up my whole life. We were happy as clams. But one morning, Kate and I woke up there in Idaho like Abraham woke up in Haran, and we knew, by the command of the Lord, that we were supposed to start a new church in Carpinteria. And that's all we knew. That's all He told us.

Later that day, after we got out of bed, I got on the phone and called my best friend, Pastor G, who worked at another church in Santa Barbara. I said, "Hey, dude, God just told us to start a church in Carpinteria."

He said, "I'm in. Tell me when."

That's all we knew. And so, because we didn't know any more, we started praying. We got some like-minded people together and started praying. Kate and I lived in Ventura at the time and we started having little prayer meetings at our house and prayed for the church. We didn't have any details; we just knew God said do it. The prayer meetings started with about five people and in a few months swelled to 150. We knew we were going to need a little more space, even just to hold the prayer meeting!

We looked around for buildings in Carpinteria and came across a big warehouse right across the street from where I went to elementary school.[2] I remember when that warehouse burned in the early eighties. My parents and I lived just a few blocks away at the time and we could see the smoke and the flames in the middle of the night as it burned. I remember hoping school would be canceled. This historic building in Carpinteria at one time was a lemon-packing factory. However, we walked into a big, scary, dank, dirty, and just plain nasty

---

2. Main Elementary School in Carpinteria, California, where I was the sixth-grade president. That was the pinnacle of my political career, thank God. It was all I could handle of politics.

empty building. We knew it would be perfect, because God told us to rent it. We met with the owners of the building and started talking with them about a lease. They wanted $16,000 a month. Now, we didn't even have a church yet, just prayer meetings. And you don't take a collection at a prayer meeting. At least we didn't, so we didn't have any money. But somehow, by the grace of God, we secured a lease for this building. With no service, no money, and a lot of financial liability, we started a church in Carpinteria just like God told us.

We still didn't have any details. We didn't know that in five years time there would be 800 people per service, multiple services in our main building, multiple campuses and Reality churches being launched around the world. God didn't tell us that. We didn't know what He would do—much less how He would do it. He didn't tell us about the building project. He didn't tell us that He would provide $1.6 million to build this place out and still be able to pay our rent and plant other churches and fully fund them. He didn't tell us any of that. He just told us to start the church. And by faith, by grace, for the glory of God, having nothing more than the command to go, we showed up on Sunday morning and God did the rest. We had faith enough to step out because we had read our Bibles. We knew that Jesus had said in Matthew 16:18, "I will build My Church." So we never had a sense about to whom this church belonged. We knew it would be His church. The weight of our decision shifted onto the person of Jesus Christ—who He is and what He said He would do. We were confident because He said it is His church. And if it's His church, then it's His problem, right? I lean on that one all the time. That's a big one for me. If it's His church, it's His problem. That's what faith is all about.

The rent back then was a lot of money, and it's way more now. But that's not our problem, not back then and still not now. God simply told us to go and He would take care of the rest. God might be telling you about things to do or places to go. It might merely be into the cubicle next to yours at work to minister to somebody. It might simply be down the hall to speak to a certain student at your school or to talk to someone in your family from whom you're estranged. Wherever it is, when God says, "Go," you need to trust Him. He's wise and He's good and He's building for His glory. And the gates of hell will not prevail over His work. You can trust in that.

When we go forth as Christians, we need to put all of our hope in Jesus Christ and nothing else. The call of the gospel is to free ourselves from self-sufficiency, from our own ingenuity, from our own where-withal, from our own worldly connections, and to put all our hope in the Word and the work of the person of Jesus Christ. In Matthew 10:37, Jesus lays it out in very strong words: "Anyone who loves his father or mother more than me is not worthy of me" (*NIV*). That's a hard one to swallow unless you really know the Lord.

Who Do You Love the Most?

I remember being a kid and driving in the car with my mom. You know how kids like to ask questions to explore and test the limits? They ask their parents questions to help them feel more secure—questions like, "Do you love me more than this?" "Do you love me more than that?" Even adults do that.

One day in particular when I was a little kid, I was riding in the car with my mom. I remember it as clear as day. We were in my mom's lit-tle Nissan Maxima station wagon, driving down Cabrillo Boulevard in downtown Santa Barbara on the way to work at the family surfboard business. It was a beautiful sunny morning just like most in Santa Bar-bara, and I was sitting in the back seat. As I looked up at the blue sky, I asked her, "Mom, do you love me more than my Huffy bike?" "Mom, do you love me more than our boat?" At first it was just surface stuff like this, but then I moved on to something a little deeper: "Mom, do you love me more than Heidi?" Heidi was my little sister. That was a big one for me.

I can't remember how Mom answered, but I'm sure she said the right thing. I must have been okay with the answer, because it was her answer to my next question that really shocked me at the time. I said, "Mom, do you love me more than God?" She looked me in the eyes and very clearly said, "No." I will never forget her response. It was one of the most profound moments in my life. I was just a little guy, and that rattled me to the core. She said to me, "I love God the most. Jesus Christ saved me, and He's the God of the universe. We need to love God the most, and then our family."

I sat there in silence for the rest of the ride into work, gazing out of my window and watching the trees go by. Her answer silenced me and shook me, but more than that, it shaped me. It really shaped my understanding of God and the priority He deserves in my life.

With my own kids now, I teach them from the youngest age that we love God the most—that Jesus Christ is the most important one over everybody else. And they get it. If you ask my five-year-old, "Who do you love most in the world, Daisy Love?" she'll say, "Jesus." She gets it.

The Myth of Security

Not only did Jesus say that we should love Him more than anyone else, He also said, "Whoever wishes to save his life will lose it, but whoever loses his life for My sake and the gospel's will save it."[3] We must surrender our lives to Him to find a life worth living, but something gets in the way—*our need to control.* Uh-oh. We all have it, don't we? We have a real need to control and to be in control, because if we feel that we're in control, then it perpetuates the myth of security in our lives. All of us have bought into that idea that we can be secure somehow—it's part of the American dream! But notice I called it the "myth" of security. It's a myth because you can never know what waits around the corner. We each create our own infrastructure and build up walls around us that appear to provide security. But no matter how hard we try, that secu-

3. Mark 8:35.

rity is just a myth. You have no idea what tomorrow holds. You may lose your job, your home, your spouse, all that you hold dear.

The security, a core ideology of Americans, so important to us is really a myth because of the unknown. And yet this sense of security causes us to take risks for our own benefit all the time. We tell ourselves, "I built up this nest egg. Therefore, I can do this for myself and I'll be okay." But simultaneously this myth of security paralyzes us from taking risks for God, because we think, "I've got it together! I have a comfortable life and a little nest egg set aside. I can't risk all that. I can't put it all on the line and go do that new thing You're calling me to do, God. I can't lay aside the family business. I can't lay aside that house. I can't lay aside these comforts." We get paralyzed by that satanic, false sense of security. And God wants to deal with that. Because the only security we can truly have is found in the person of Jesus Christ and the gospel of God, the only real security. As Christians we need to be willing to take risks according to *that* reality—risks that bring glory to God and benefit His kingdom, instead of benefiting us.

What's the Plan, Lord?

By all accounts in the Bible, Abraham enjoyed great wealth. There's nothing wrong with being wealthy. But God needed to deal with his need to control. So God said, "Go." Abraham had a natural response: "Where am I going?" God told him, "Bro, just chill." Okay, I'm paraphrasing; He didn't really say that. He said, "I'm not going to tell you where; I simply told you to go." So Abraham went. You see, Abraham didn't need all the info or all the answers to obey. That's a real lesson for us. Abraham understood. He didn't demand all the info or all the answers to obey God. That's trust. That's surrender. God wants to deal with our need to control. We must realize Abraham didn't get any answers *until he obeyed*. Once he obeyed, *then* he received understanding. Yet so many of us today sit paralyzed by this satanic false sense of security, saying, "God, I need answers." That precludes us from simple obedience—because we're demanding answers that God isn't obligated to give. We need to learn from Abraham's example: when he went, he just walked out the door, *then* he discovered, by the leading of the Holy Spirit, that his destination was Canaan.

A lot of Christians will tell you their favorite verse is Jeremiah 29:11: " 'For I know the plans I have for you,' declares the Lord, 'plans to prosper you and not to harm you, plans to give you a hope and a future' " (*NIV*). That's a good verse. It's one of those security verses. We feel like God will take care of us. Many Christians claim the promise in that verse, failing to recognize that God was speaking to the nation of Israel when they were in exile in Babylon. Still, it speaks of God's character and the reality that He cares for His people.

Here's another thing we often miss about that part of Scripture. When God says, "I know the plans I have for you," we immediately say, "Awesome, Lord! Tell me the plans." That's immediately where we go. "Oh, You know the plans, Lord? Perfect. I've been wondering what the plans were. Speak to me, Lord. Tell me the plans." But notice the next two verses in Jeremiah 29:12-13. Immediately after saying "I know the plans I have for you," God says:

Then you will call upon Me and come and pray to Me, and I will listen to you. You will seek Me and find Me when you search for Me with all your heart.

So the discerning Christian now realizes, "Oh, wait a minute. It's not about the plans. *God* is the plan." Now that's a paradigm shift. God is saying, "I know the plans I have for you. Don't worry about it. You come and call on *Me*. You come and pray to *Me*. You come and seek *Me* and you'll find *Me* when you search for *Me* with all your heart." And when we find Him, we find the plan, because *Jesus Christ is the plan*. We get all caught up in the details, demanding to know the step-by-step when it's very simple: God is the goal.

Give Me the Details

Remember, Jesus said the first and greatest commandment is to love the Lord your God with all your heart, soul, mind and strength. Everything else is detail. But we want to know the details, don't we? That creates a disconnect in our lives. We think that knowing the details will make us feel secure. If we don't find security in Jesus Christ alone, it's false and will keep us from going when God says to go. You see, God isn't your genie in a bottle. He does not exist to give you answers. He is the glorious, sovereign, holy, awesome, terrifying God of the universe. His very nature commands worship and obedience. Who are we to stand on the earth and shake our fists at God and say, "I won't go until You tell me the details!" We all do it. We spend an exorbitant amount of time asking why, when and where.

We are often more *demanding* of God than *trusting* in God. Yet Jesus calls us to a childlike faith—a faith that simply trusts in the Father. If you have kids, you remember being in a pool teaching them how to swim. They're standing on the edge and you say, "Come on, jump to Daddy!" Our heavenly Father rejoices when His kid just goes for it and jumps into His arms, right? That same father *despairs* when the same kid comes to a point when he just won't jump with joyful abandon anymore. After a brief, but sometimes intense, exchange, the merciful father goes to the edge of the pool. He holds the child's little hands and eases him in. He is patient and kind. That doesn't negate the silliness of that child for thinking that his father is going to let him drown in three feet of water. We do that to our Father God. He's so much bigger than all of our circumstances, yet we stand on the edge and say, "No, God, no! What if I drown? When, why, where? You have to show me." Still, the Father says, "Come."

Enjoy the Ride

We are to trust the Father with a childlike faith. Not a *childish* faith. There's a big difference. Childlike faith trusts the Father and jumps off the edge, right into His arms—never a thought that your Father would ever drop you. A childish faith, on the other hand, complains and moans and groans, when you're supposed to be enjoying the ride.

When I was a kid, my family used to drive to Mammoth Mountain a lot to go skiing. My sister and I would both sit in the backseat, and before long, my dad would try to keep one hand on the steering wheel as he swung his other arm behind him, trying to swat us while shouting, "I'll pull this car over right now! Get on your side! Get over there!" I remember leaning back as far as I could, and I could get *just* out of his reach. Of course, we knew of the constant threat of him pulling over, and really reaching in the back seat and giving it to us. Because what were we kids doing? We were teasing each other and bickering and whining and asking my dad all kinds of questions.

The quintessential one was, of course, "Are we there yet?" every three seconds. And it drives parents nuts. As an adult with a little bit of understanding and maturity, things are different. You're cruising down the road and it's beautiful. You're on your way to Mammoth. The scenery is nice and the music is on. Your wife sits next to you and she's gorgeous. Everything is cool and you're enjoying the ride. Then the whining starts up from the back seat. You think, "You silly kid. Why can't you just enjoy the ride? We'll get there and when we do it's going to be awesome. But for now can you just enjoy the ride for a minute?" But they can't because they're childish.

In the same way, so many Christians are childish—in the back seat, whining and complaining to the Father: "Are we there yet? Why aren't we there? What's going on?" And the Father says, "My son, my daughter, can you be quiet and enjoy the ride? I'm doing good things in your life. Can you stop worrying and just enjoy My company? Can you open your eyes to where you are and see the beauty of where I have you right now?" God wants you to enjoy the ride. And He Himself is the destination anyway. So there's no sense in asking, "Are we there yet?" because if we are with Him, we're there.

Willing to Forego

We know Abraham went without knowing where. He also was willing to forego according to what he *did* know. Faith is willing to forego permanency in this world, because faith lives for the future reality. Again, Hebrews 11:1 says, "Faith is the assurance of things hoped for, the conviction of things not seen." It has to do with the unseen realm and future realities guaranteed us in the Word and work and ultimately in the person of Jesus Christ. Abraham was willing to forego certain things in this world according to what he knew about the world to come. He lived for more than the immediate. That's the heavenly and eternal Jerusalem that Hebrews 11:10 is referring to when it says, "For he [Abraham] was looking for a city which has foundations, whose architect and builder is God." And Abraham is pictured as a pilgrim in this current life, living in the light of that reality to come. It says in Hebrews 11:9:

> By faith he lived as an alien in the land of promise, as in a foreign land, dwelling in tents with Isaac and Jacob, fellow heirs of the same promise.

Abraham was convinced of and fixated on an eternal reality with God. And so in this life, his dwelling place was a tent. A tent speaks of the idea of just passing through, just staying for a little while. And this is a picture of a pilgrim. Now a pilgrim is not a drifter, because a pilgrim has a set and certain goal. They don't aimlessly wander around whichever way the wind blows. A pilgrim has a destination in mind. And the problem with us as Christians is that too many of our set and certain goals are wrapped up in the here and now. We're only convinced about the value of the present. But Jesus said, "In My Father's house are many mansions; if it were not so, I would have told you. I go to prepare a place for you. And if I go and prepare a place for you, I will come again and receive you to Myself; that where I am, there you may be also."[4] He promises us a better heavenly dwelling and a place of reward

---

4. John 14:2-3, *NKJV.*

according to faithfulness, and yet we so quickly and easily get wrapped up in building our mansions today. Now there's nothing wrong with a mansion. If you have a mansion, that's awesome. Invite me over for dinner. There's no problem with having a big house in this world. We just need to make sure that in this life we are more interested in being rich toward God than we are in being rich in the here and now.

What's in It for Me?

Peter knew what it meant to leave behind some things to follow Jesus. In Mark 10:28, he complained to Jesus, saying, "We have left everything and followed You." You can sense that he thought, *What's in it for me? You showed up one day there when I was washing my nets and said follow Me. Well, I left the nets, I left the boats, I left the family business and now I'm following You. So what's going to be in this for me?* Jesus, knowing his heart, responds in Mark 10:29-31:

> Truly I say to you, there is no one who has left house or brothers or sisters or mother or father or children or farms, for My sake and for the gospel's sake, but that he will receive a hundred times as much now in the present age, houses and brothers and sisters and mothers and children and farms, along with persecutions; and in the age to come, eternal life. But many who are first will be last, and the last, first.

In this passage, Jesus lays out what's in it for us when we leave things behind to follow Him. First, He gives us a caveat: We have to do it for *His* sake and for the sake of the gospel. Then He gives us the promise that we will receive many times more—and receive it "now in the present age," meaning that the kingdom of God begins here and now. Then He just kind of drops in that little phrase "along with persecutions." Oops. The name-it-and-claim-it crowd really likes the first part of that verse, but not so much the second part. You can hear the prayer now: "Lord, I'm claiming my hundred houses!" But you never hear someone pray for a hundredfold persecution. "Lord, give the brother a hundredfold persecution!" Nobody says that.

Finally, Jesus said that in the age to come we will receive eternal life. He adds, "But many who are first will be last and the last shall be first." Essentially, He was saying, "Peter, you need to reverse your thinking. You're caught up in the here and now. You're looking for a temporal reward. But there's something bigger, there's something more to live for and I'm telling you that I am going to prepare a place for you. And it's going to be wonderful, and I'm going to come to receive you, that there you may be also."

Let's get our eyes and our hearts and our affections freed from the things of this world and set on the things of God. It doesn't mean that we're going to lose everything in this world. It *might* mean that. Remember that God is a giver, not a taker. It reminds me of a popular bumper sticker back in the 1980s: "He who dies with the most toys wins." Well that thought is about as anti-Christian as it can get. There is something called the Bema Seat, the judgment seat of Christ. A time is coming when we will stand before Jesus Christ and give an account for what we did with the time, talents, connections, friends, family and resources that God gave us. We will stand before Jesus Christ—the One who has the royal diadems upon His head and whose eyes are a flaming fire—and we will answer for how we used this life. Was it for His glory or for our own? Nobody's going to lose his salvation at that point. This judgment is for a reward. But there will be many who see their life's work (and toys) burn up as wood, hay and stubble, as 1 Corinthians 3:11-15 speaks of, because it was for their own selfish desires and not God's glory. A lot of what might be fun in this lifetime will ultimately be meaningless.

We need to constantly remember that the life to come is a lot longer than this one. How foolish would it be to trade such a long and glorious eternity for a little fun in this short life? At some point the Christian has to say, "Okay, life isn't about me. It's about Jesus Christ.

He's given me gifts and talents and resources to glorify Him in this world for a short time, and I'm going to do that. He's probably not going to tell me all of the details; He's not going to give me the play-by-play. He's just going to say go. And when He does, I'm going to go and I'm going to do it for His glory." The Bible promises that there is a reward in the life to come, and that's how Abraham was living. Abraham was willing to forego according to what he did know. He was willing to forego that façade of security, to pass up putting down deep roots, and building in this life for this life. He was willing to forego the passing pleasures of this world for the lasting joys of the world to come. You see, a pilgrim keeps the lightest touch on this world and has a certain and set goal: a better life in the world to come. A pilgrim endeavors to be rich toward God and to build something that will last.[5]

It's What You *Want* to Do

There's another kind of pilgrimage that Christians are required to make. When any person comes to Christ, God demands of that person a pilgrimage from his or her old pattern of living into a new way of life. Things should change in that person's life when he or she chooses to follow Jesus. I mean, let's not soft sell this thing. There should be transformation, because God is all about transformation.[6]

When real change happens in our lives, that's a pilgrimage from the old ways of thinking and doing into the new ways. One of the biggest obstacles to the life of faith is the old way of living and the refusal to let those old things go. For many, worldliness impedes the life of faith. We want to hold on to the old life. It's an attitude, not necessarily an act. It's *wanting* to do things that are sinful, selfish or worthless, whether we actually do them or not. It's *wanting* fame, praise, recognition, reputation and stuff, whether we ever get those things or not. It's holding to high

---

5. See The Parable of the Rich Fool in Luke 12:16-31.
6. See Romans 12:1-2.

standards of conduct outwardly, but inwardly longing to live like the rest of the world. It's hypocrisy. Worldliness is not so much what we do, it's what we want to do. It's an issue of the heart.

What keeps us from actually *doing* those things might be a fear of the consequences, a concern for what others would think, self-righteousness, or whatever. But all the while, our hearts hold on to that strong desire to do those wrong things. It's a heart issue. Jesus dealt with this in the Sermon on the Mount, His kingdom manifesto. He said, "You have heard that it was said to the people long ago, 'Do not murder,' and 'anyone who murders will be subject to judgment.' But I tell you that anyone who is angry with his brother will be subject to judgment."[7] It's always an issue of the heart.

Worldliness is an attitude in which a person really *wants* to live like the unredeemed world, but in actuality doesn't—often just out of hypocrisy.[8] This was the sin of the Pharisees. But Christians who are really walking with God discover they can do whatever they want to do in this life. That's the mark of spiritual maturity. The mature Christian finds that he or she *wants* to do things that glorify God. There's less of that inner conflict going on.

As I meditated on this definition of worldliness, I realized that I'm a lot more worldly than I want to be. There really is something inside of me that wants to live like the rest of the world, but says, "Well, I'm a pastor, so I can't. I'm a Christian, so I can't." There are all these reasons that I can't—even though I really want to. Now I've repented of this before God, and perhaps you need to as well, because God looks upon the heart. And it's this worldliness that keeps us from an authentic life of faith. Even though we may never act upon it, the inner *desire* to do wrong is the root from which we need to sever ourselves. To overcome we must fall more in love with Jesus and to see Him as more desirable

---

7. Matthew 5:21-22, *NIV*.

8. The following is adapted from John MacArthur, Jr., *The MacArthur New Testament Commentary (Hebrews)* (Chicago, IL: Moody Press, 1983), pp. 328-329.

than anything the world has to offer. I've found that we can't force ourselves to be good—and we're not called to. We are called to be transformed by the Holy Spirit through a loving, meaningful relationship with Jesus Christ. When we change the object of our love and desire, it will vanquish worldliness and we will easily and happily forego certain things according to what we do know: the future with Jesus Christ.

Worship and Witness

First, Abraham went without knowing where. Second, he was willing to forego certain things based on what he did know. Third, he had the willingness to worship and witness. He knew the same truth that the Westminster catechism states: "The chief end of man is to glorify God and enjoy Him forever." That is the meaning of life. Abraham understood this and therefore was willing to worship God in His glory and to witness of His glory.

One way of glorifying God is just enjoying Him and who He is. As John Piper says, "God is most glorified in us when we are most satisfied in Him."[9] When you're satisfied in Jesus Christ, you can do whatever you want to do in this lifetime, because your desires change. The most mature Christian is the one who does exactly what he wants to do because he's so in love with Jesus Christ that he doesn't want to do anything contrary to Christ's character.

Since Abraham had seen God's power and recognized His supremacy, he trusted God completely and was willing to worship and to witness in a confrontational way to both popular culture and the false gods of the day. This is big. In Genesis 12:6 it says that Abraham went to the oak of Moreh—the place where all the Canaanite soothsayers gathered.[10] "Moreh" means "teacher" or "oracle giver." So the people who had a desire to know the future—a desire that is still very prevalent

---

9. John Piper, *Desiring God* (Sisters, OR: Multnomah, 2003), p. 258.
10. Soothsayers were people who claimed to know the future apart from God.

today—these people would come to hear what the soothsayers had to say there at the oak of Moreh. The soothsayers would listen to the rustling of the leaves on the oak tree and then say, "Well, here's what the leaves tell us about the future."[11] It's interesting that the oak of Moreh and the place it was in, Shechem, were right at the geographical center of Canaan. So Abraham went right to the middle of the Promised Land, directly to where these false prophets were in business. And check out what happened next.

Genesis 12:7 says that the Lord appeared to Abraham there! As far as we know, the Lord had never appeared to him before—Abraham had only heard God's voice. And in response, he built an altar to the Lord. He didn't just say a quick "Praise the Lord" or "Amen." Abraham built an altar right there at the oak of Moreh! He was willing to worship God in a way that was confrontational to the prevailing culture. And he didn't do it because he disliked the people, but because we wage war against powers and principalities and spiritual forces of wickedness in high places. He must have recognized some falsehood there, some spiritual business exalting itself against the one true God who alone knows the beginning from the end. And so Abraham confronted the culture with the reality of worship, and built an altar to God right there in the midst of it.

God Is Already There

Abraham stepped into a world dominated by people who did not know the God of the Bible and were not seeking Him. But Abraham discovered that *God was already there*, confronting the idols, the false religions and the lies of the Canaanites.

It's no different in your life. God is already on mission around you—at your workplace, at your school, amongst your friends, in your family. He's already there, confronting falsehood and every other evil thing.

---

11. R. Kent Hughes, *Preaching the Word: Hebrews,* vol. 2 (Wheaton, IL: Crossway Books, 1993), p. 186.

And if we would just be willing to join God in confronting culture by exalting Jesus Christ, we would see more of God in our workplaces, schools and communities. It will happen when we get into God's mission and exalt Jesus Christ above the drama of the world.

One way the Lord has allowed our church to confront culture with worship happens every year at the biggest thing that happens in our little town, Carpinteria's Avocado Festival. Every year the city asks us to come on Sunday morning and do church. They *ask* us to come and build an altar of praise at the oak of Moreh. We set up the biggest sound system we can find, we turn it up to 11, and we preach and worship Jesus right there in the middle of town. And when a couple thousand people worship and proclaim Jesus boldly and passionately in the open air in the geographic, social and financial center in a city of only 14,000, something happens.

I believe that as we worship Jesus Christ at the oak of Moreh like Abraham did, the soothsayers are put on notice—the purveyors of lies, like the fortuneteller who wanted to open up shop on our main street, and the peddlers of deception and false religions that don't lift Jesus up. When we proclaim and praise Jesus there, the lies come down and strongholds are broken. The forces that want to rip off our kids and steal from our community and destroy our marriages and break apart the fabric of society—they are shattered when we confront them with the supremacy of Jesus Christ. But we can't just do it once a year, as a big church gathered. Each of us must do it every day when we are the church scattered, in our own lives, on our own turf, where we live and work and play. And we must do it to the glory of God.

Go Big and Go Public

Not only did Abraham confront culture with worship, but he was also willing to witness. It says in Genesis 12:8 that he went to a place called Bethel and called upon the name of the Lord. Abraham went directly to where the chief god of Canaan was worshiped and he called upon the name of the Lord. And in the Mosaic writings, when it says "called upon the name of the Lord," it generally means that he *proclaimed* the name of the Lord. Abraham was now witnessing about, testifying of, the one true God.

Now, Abraham didn't just show up by himself. He rolled into Bethel with a big entourage—his family and Lot and all their stuff and all their people. The locals knew exactly where he was and what he was doing at all times. And he went straight to the temple, to where their primary god resided, and began to proclaim the name of Yahweh in that place. Why? Because "The chief end of man is to glorify God and enjoy Him forever." Abraham had heard and seen God and, like the disciples said in Acts 4:20 before the threatening religious leaders of that day, "we cannot stop speaking about what we have seen and heard." Abraham knew whom he had believed and entrusted himself to and he had faith that was willing to witness. Thus he joined in and continued the *misseo dei* of glorifying God among the nations. Are you willing to do the same in your context? In your place? Where God has you? Such is the life of faith.

Abraham's faith made him willing to go, even when he didn't have all the answers. His faith made him willing to forego the passing pleasures of this world, so he could live for something more lasting: the city made by God. And finally, Abraham's faith made him willing to worship and witness at the pivotal places God had him, confronting culture with the reality of Jesus Christ. May we be men and women who are like Abraham, proclaiming God's name and building altars of praise wherever we go. May our faith be willing.

ON A RECENT TRIP HOME FROM LONDON,
I was reminded how much waiting is involved when you travel. I couldn't wait to return home after a long, cold trip. The day before I left for London, I laid in the sun on the beach near my home. So when I arrived in England, all I had on were my Vans and my jeans and my standard black T-shirt. I wasn't ready for the below-freezing temperatures there—the temperature never got above 32 degrees, and the biggest snowstorm in 18 years blasted the city. I couldn't wait to get back to sunny Carpinteria. But it takes forever!

When you get to the airport to check in, you have to wait in line. You get through the line at check-in, give them your luggage, and then you wait in the line to get through security. At security, you have to take off your jacket, shoes and belt. You're almost naked by the time you get through the metal detector! Then there's frisking before you get through, and then it's onto the gate, where you wait some more. Finally, you begin to board—but if you have a seat at the back of the plane, like I had, you have to wait until they call your boarding zone.

When that happens, you walk down the little jetway—and, of course, by this point a line has formed. In London the jetways are not heated, so you wait in below-freezing temps in the tunnel as people struggle with their carry-on luggage. When you finally get inside the plane, you wait again while people try to cram their nine carry-ons (well, maybe that's an exaggeration) into the overhead compartments. At long last you sit down, get situated with all your stuff, and buckle up. (I'm six-foot-six, so my knees are always nailed against the seat in front of me.)

Now you wait for the plane to taxi to the runway. A voice comes over the loudspeaker: "Hello, and welcome to Virgin Atlantic. We are currently ninety-seventh for takeoff today, so we'll be underway in just a few hours." When you finally get into the air, you're up there for a long time coming home from London. (Some guy on my flight had a medical emergency, so we had to land in Maine. When we landed they wanted to refuel, so we had to wait for two hours. At long last we took off again, but we still had six hours before landing at LAX.)

So you finally arrive at your destination. But wait—then they announce, "There's some traffic on the runway, so we'll have to wait a little while to get to our gate." So you wait to get to the gate. When you get to the gate and pull up to the jetway, you have to wait for them to turn off the seatbelt sign. When that little light goes off, all the passengers open their seatbelts at the same time with one big simultaneous CLICK! Everybody stands up and grabs their luggage. Guess what? Now you wait, standing there forever, holding your nine carry-ons, waiting to get off the plane. When you get off, you head straight to customs, where you have to wait in another line.

That line is the worst. I think paint dries faster than that line moves. I finally got to the front with my little form, all filled out. I had read the form carefully, and it didn't say that I had to fill it out in blue or black ink. I specifically checked, because all I had with me on the plane was a pink pen. So I filled it out with a pink pen. When I got to the customs counter, the guy said, "Sorry, but you can't use a pink pen." He sent me to the back of the line with a new form and a black pen. So I filled it out for the second time and waited in the line—again. I got through customs and went to baggage claim to wait for my bags. After retrieving my checked bag, I went outside and waited at the curb for the shuttle.

I learned one thing on that trip: I hate traveling. And the only reason I hate it is because of all the waiting.

The Work of Waiting

I think the reason we don't like to wait is that waiting feels like work. Perhaps that is because there *is* a work that is accomplished in waiting—if we are waiting on God. God works in us to change and improve us while we're waiting on Him. He works into us certain things that He wants to see in our lives. He purges out certain things that ought not to be there. He matures us. He tempers and balances us. The result is greater character in our lives. We begin to live with deeper integrity and a higher level of trust, resolve and motivation. God shapes these qualities in us through the process of waiting on Him. That's why waiting is an inescapable part of the Christian life! God *wants* us to wait. As Isaiah 55:8 says, God's ways are not our ways, and, lo and behold, God's timing is not our timing! We will all find ourselves, from time to time, waiting on God.

Abraham and Sarah's life together exemplifies a faith of waiting. The reality is that they had a difficult time waiting on God. (To be fair, they had to wait 25 years for God to fulfill the promise that He made.) While they waited, they made a monumental mistake and also had some very revealing moments. But, in spite of their stumbling, we can learn much about faith through their lives—particularly from Sarah.

As we consider Abraham and Sarah in Hebrews 11:11, we start out by recognizing that in the original Greek there are some ambiguities in the grammar that make it unclear who the subject of the sentence is. We're not sure from the original Greek whether it's about Sarah or Abraham. Of the 20 English translations I reviewed, the *New International Version* and the *New Century Version* have Abraham as the subject. The *NIV* reads:

> By faith Abraham, even though he was past age—and Sarah herself was barren—was enabled to become a father because he considered him faithful who had made the promise.

The explicit mention of Sarah in this passage is clearly a commendation of her faith. Both of them needed to have faith when God promised them a child—the fulfillment of their greatest dream. The lesson from this text is the same: Abraham and Sarah's lives of faith exemplify faith that is waiting.

Abel exemplified faith that is worshiping. Enoch exemplified faith that is walking. Noah exemplified faith that is working. Abraham exemplified faith that is willing. In this chapter, Sarah's life teaches us about faith that is waiting. This follows the Holy Spirit's progression of things: Worship comes first; faith that worships will also walk; faith that walks will also work; faith that worships, walks and works is willing, and faith that is willing will sometimes have to wait.

We Hate to Wait

Abraham and Sarah had a hard time waiting on God. Waiting for 25 years for God to fulfill His promise would be hard for anyone! Hopefully very few of us will have to wait that long, because most of us are only good for about two weeks before we start losing it. Abraham and Sarah ultimately made it through the wait, but they didn't always do that great while they waited. They made one huge misstep and had a few other embarrassing incidents along the way. But that's true of almost all the people in Hebrews 11. They experienced ups and downs. They had days when they had strong faith and other days when they were really weak and their faith failed them. They were just like us. And just like us, they didn't like to wait.

How to Wait on God

We have a right way and a wrong way to wait on God. The correct way is to wait *without being passive*. Second, we need to wait *without causing problems*. Third, we need to wait *without missing God's promises*. That's how we wait on God. There's an incredible story in Genesis 15:1-6 that is alluded to later in Hebrews 11. This story shows us why it is so important to wait without being passive. It begins with God promising Abraham a son:

> After these things the word of the LORD came to Abram in a vision, saying, "Do not fear, Abram, I am a shield to you; Your reward shall be very great." Abram said, "O Lord GOD, what will You give me, since I am childless, and the heir of my house is Eliezer of Damascus?" And Abram said, "Since You have given

no offspring to me, one born in my house is my heir." Then behold, the word of the LORD came to him, saying, "This man will not be your heir; but one who will come forth from your own body, he shall be your heir." And He took him outside and said, "Now look toward the heavens, and count the stars, if you are able to count them." And He said to him, "So shall your descendants be." Then he believed in the LORD; and He reckoned it to him as righteousness.

God promises Abraham a son—indeed many sons, an innumerable amount of offspring. This promise is given to Abraham at age 75. Think about it: he doesn't have any kids yet and God says, "Abraham, you're not just going to have a son, but your offspring will be as numerous as the stars in heaven." By faith he believed the Lord when he received the promise—even at 75 years old! I don't know any 75-year-olds who would say, "Oh, yeah, I'm still gonna have a bunch of kids." But Abraham had faith.

What Are You Waiting For?

As the story unfolds, we find Abraham and Sarah would have to wait *25 years* for the fulfillment of that promise. But remember, what they were waiting for was God's promise—what God said He would do. At one time or another, we have all waited on God for something. What have you waited for? What are you waiting for now?

First, we must be sure we are waiting on God, on His promises and nothing else. We need to be clear on the object of our faith, and we need to be certain of the promise that God has made. This thing that you're waiting for and looking forward to—is it God's call? Is it His plan? Is it His purpose? Is it His mission? Or is it your own? Because if it's our own, then we can't really say we're waiting on God. We hear it all the time, but often it's just empty Christianese when people say they are "waiting on God." If we're going to be biblically correct, waiting on God means that there is some promise, some word you've received from Him concerning His plan, His purpose, His call and His mission for you.

Abraham and Sarah had a clear promise from God. This promise would affect and bless them, to be sure. But in the final analysis, it wasn't about them. We need to get this, because we tend to make waiting on God about us. The promise of children to Abraham and Sarah was about God's plan and purpose to reveal Himself and to bless all the nations through Israel and ultimately through the Messiah. When God works in our lives, He wants to accomplish *His* purposes, not ours.

A disconnect often takes place around this idea—that God is working on His purposes through our lives—because our time scale is simply too small. We get caught up in the here and now, and soon all we can see is what's going to affect us right now. For us, long-term thinking is the length of our lifetime—70 or 80 years maybe. Very seldom do we think beyond that. Mostly, we think about what's going to affect us today, this week, this year. God's promises to Abraham and Sarah would take *thousands* of years to unfold, from the birth of their son Isaac, to the formation of the nation of Israel, to the Messiah coming from Israel and blessing the nations, to all the nations being redeemed and ultimately gathered around the throne of God, offering worship to the person of Jesus Christ. We can't see that far out because we're almost hopelessly myopic. That's the disconnect. We can only see what's right in front of us. But God is way bigger than that. And God's purposes are bigger than our lifespan, bigger than our life. God might be working things in and through you today that will affect generations.

We have to start looking at things from God's time scale and make sure that we're not missing God's purpose. Our time scale is too small.

False Gospel, False Expectations

Failing to realize that it's all about God's purposes—and not our own—breeds false expectations. We think it's about us. And so we set up these false expectations that become very problematic for our emotional security and stability. In his great book about evil and suffering, D. A. Carson said, "Much mental suffering is tied to our false expectations. We may so link our hopes and joys and future to a new job, to a promotion, to certain kinds of success, to prosperity, that when they fail to materialize, we are utterly crushed. But quiet confidence in God alone breeds stability and delight amid 'all the changing scenes of life.'"[1]

Now this is especially poignant for us. We have been poisoned by a false gospel in this nation, the prosperity gospel, which tells us that it's all about your health and it's all about your wealth. That's a totally egocentric theology and it's false! It feeds into our fallen selfish nature and our consumerism as Americans. And what's worse is that we have the audacity as Americans to export this corrupt theology to places like Thailand and Africa where there's real suffering and a great need for the truth. But it's endemic within our culture to think we have certain inalienable rights from God and we *deserve* something. That belief sets up false expectations and is sure to bring disappointment.

We have to ask ourselves in our times of waiting if we are really waiting on God or just some idea that we've proposed to God—or, worse, if we are demanding something from God with a sense of entitlement. *We have no rights!* Our rights were done away with when Jesus Christ was nailed to the cross. When we come to Him, we surrender. We surrender all, not just what we feel like, including our self-righteous promises. We don't deserve anything. Scripture is very clear about what we deserve: We deserve hell, and it is only by the grace of God that we can avoid it. It's only because of what Jesus did on the cross, not because of any right of our own.

It's essential to realize that God's promises have to do with the person of Jesus Christ and not the person of us. It's about Him and His

---

1. D. A. Carson, *How Long O Lord: Reflections on Evil and Suffering* (Grand Rapids. MI: Baker Books, 1990), p. 242.

glory and His mission. So often, waiting is frustrating because we're waiting on our own plans or purposes.

Waiting Without Being Passive

We need to be sure that we're waiting on God for His plans and His purposes. Once we've established that, we need to realize that our faith is to be an *active* faith. Waiting on God never means paralysis. It's not like waiting in an airport, where at best you can read a book or watch a movie. When we wait on God, we are to be engaged with God. We don't just sit back, do nothing and say, "Okay, God, You said You were gonna do this, so I'm just gonna sit here and wait for You to do it." That's not what it means to wait on God.

Our faith is to be active, not passive. That means we're to study the Word of God—and seek the God of the Word. We're to be thoroughly engaged, worshiping, praying, asking and seeking. We'll find Jesus when we do these things. When our prayer life increases and our Bible study increases and our worship life increases, we discover that it's all about Jesus in the final analysis. So everything else becomes peripheral and it gets easier to wait because we're already working towards the goal, which is knowing Him! Knowing and loving Jesus Christ is the goal of our existence. And when He has us in a posture of waiting, if we refuse to be passive, and seek and ask and press in through prayer and worship, we will find Him. And in that moment, the soul is settled. Abraham had to wait 25 years, but in the final analysis the Bible says that he was a friend of God. The totality of his life was not summarized by the fact that he waited, but by the fact that he was a friend of the living God. That's what life is about.

One of my best friends in the whole world—let's call him Bo—went through a difficult time financially. Bo had a great job, made lots of money and worked from home. He had lots of flexibility, and made his own schedule. That's something many people wish for. Because of a downturn in the economy, he lost his job. On top of that, he had gone pretty much all in on this one big investment. That investment went bad and he lost all of that money. So now he and his wife and their two kids were faced with losing their home.

I know a lot of people are much worse off than that. For Bo and his family, it has been painful to simultaneously lose a job, a big investment and then a home. So I checked on him, and was amazed when he said that he had peace just waiting on God. Bo's well respected in his field, and could call up some previous employers and get another job immediately. But God told him not to. God told him to wait because something new would happen in his life. So he didn't make that phone call to get a new job.

So I asked about the ins and outs of waiting on God. Bo started with the negative as we often do. Should he have made that investment? Or what if he called an old employer? He admitted to the pain of playing every scenario over and over in his head. Then he said, "But, when I get back to the place where I experience the peace of God, it takes all the anxiety and fearful thoughts away."

I said, "Okay, cool. That's good. But how do you get to the place where you're experiencing the peace of God?"

He replied, "I go away and I pray. I go up to the mountains, sit on a certain rock and pray to the Lord—out loud, in the Spirit, any way that I can think of. It takes me about a full hour of doing that before I really feel like I have shut out all the noise, all the self-talk, all my fearful thoughts. And then I just sit there, being still before God. That's where I find my peace, and I find that my level of peace is in direct correlation to my prayer life."

In Philippians 4:6, Paul says the same thing: "Be anxious for nothing, but in everything by prayer and supplication with thanksgiving let your requests be made known to God." The *New Living Translation* states it this way: "Don't worry about anything; instead, pray about everything. Tell God what you need, and thank him for all he has done." So we should start out by praising God, and then tell Him everything that's going on. Look at the promise we're given in verse 7:

"And the peace of God, which surpasses all comprehension, will guard your hearts and your minds in Christ Jesus."

Bo continued his testimony, saying, "As I've been practicing prayer, I've been experiencing peace. My heart and mind, which are full of anxiety, have been guarded in Christ Jesus." The degree of peace we experience really is tied to our prayer lives. D.A. Carson explains, "This is not because prayer is psychologically soothing, but because we address a prayer-answering God, a personal God, a responding God, a sovereign God whom we can trust with the outcomes of life's confusion."[2] That's who God really is.

"Okay, tell me more," I said. "What else do you do?"

Bo said, "Well, while I'm waiting on God, I've discovered that I have to repeatedly surrender."

"What do you mean repeatedly?" I asked.

He answered, "I find I have to surrender the same things over and over. I'll surrender something one time and then here it comes again and I have to surrender it all over again. And I also have to practice progressive surrender."

"Progressive surrender?" I asked. "What is that?"

He said, "The more I surrender, the more things I discover I need to surrender. There are things in my life I didn't even know were a problem until I began to surrender other things. That's when I realize that I need to surrender them too. So the more I surrender, the more I discover I need to surrender, so the more I surrender. And the more I surrender . . . progressive surrender."

"Britt, I Am Not Your Secretary"

Bo also told me he kept track of what God said by journaling. God used to speak to me in the middle of the night. He used to wake me up and tell me cool things. I never wrote it down because it was in the

---

2. D. A. Carson, *How Long O Lord: Reflections on Evil and Suffering*, p. 242.

middle of the night. I didn't want to be bothered. I had this funky theology about that. God would wake me up and He'd speak to me and show me some cool stuff and I'd say to myself, "Wow, that's really gonna be applicable to my life and other people's lives. Maybe I should write it down." Instead of writing it down I figured "God will remind me." So I'd go back to bed and in the morning I'd wake up and say, "Okay, God, what was that again?" I could never remember, and that would frustrate me. One time, I said, "Lord, what's the deal? Remind me of what You told me!" Quickly He said, "Britt, I am not your secretary. When I speak, you write it down." Needless to say, the next time God spoke to me, I was ready to write it down.

God has been speaking to Bo too, and he's been writing it all down. And something else that he's been doing—something that's profound and totally right on—is that he's been paying closer attention to the Body of Christ. He's been listening to what people in the Body of Christ would want to speak into his life by the Spirit of God. And he's also paying closer attention to the Word of God. Reading through the Bible in a year is a whole new gig for him now. Bo has been listening for God's prophetic voice, listening to God's corporate voice as He speaks through the Body of Christ, and listening for the voice of God in the written word.

It's All on Purpose

Bo also says that he saturates himself in the presence of God. Any time there's worship at church, he'll show up. He worships in his house, too. He also gets alone with God like never before. He says that he also tries to be more "others-focused," because in his waiting, he has found there is a real tendency to get self-centered and consumed with his own situation. Bo realizes, through the story of Scripture, that God has a purpose that is bigger than his own drama. Knowing that God is bigger—that God is working a bigger plan—has removed Bo's anxiety and brought him security. He has discovered that God is a God of purpose and that any time spent waiting on God is not wasted time. Waiting is work, but waiting does work. When we're waiting on God, there's a work that is accomplished in us because He's a purposeful God.

Enjoying the Process

While waiting, Bo asked the Lord, "What would You have me do? What's my next step?" He would not stray to the right or to the left without marching orders from God. And you know what he's heard God say over and over again? "Just wait. Wait a little more." But he says this, "What I'm discovering is Jesus, and falling so much more in love with the Lord, experiencing so much of Him that I don't really care so much about the outcome anymore. I'm just finding more of Jesus in my life."

So you see, I think my friend Bo did it right. He waited on God without being passive, and discovered what we need to discover: that God is all about the process. That's really important for our lives. We're all about the goal but God is all about the process. Because of that there's a disconnect between us and God. I can see this disconnect as I try to follow a plan to read through the Bible in a year. In fact, I used to refuse to do it because I am so goal-oriented. What happens is, if I know I need to read four chapters today, I get two chapters into it and start thinking, *Okay, two chapters down, two chapters to go. I'm gettin' this baby done right now.* God just wants us to sit with Him as we read His Word, but I'm so goal-oriented that I would miss God.

As a people, we tend to be like this. We're so goal-oriented, so conditioned this way in our culture, that we miss God in the process. And God is all about the process. While Abraham and Sarah were waiting 25 years for God to fulfill His Word, God was working in them. The same is true for us. If God has us waiting, it's because He is working, not because He is too busy. It's not a cosmic "take a number" thing. It's not as though God gives us a promise and says, "Okay, now, I gave you My promise. I'll check back in with you in 25 years." That's not who God is.

God Is in the Details

I believe God deals with me even in my sleep, in my thoughts and dreams, at the subconscious level. God is always dealing with His people, and God is all about the process. A common, modern view of God has Him involved in just the big things—the major turning points of history—but not necessarily the details of our lives. Much of our own theology is based on a similar view. It's probably not spoken theology. We wouldn't *say* that because we know the Bible says otherwise. But it is often our practical theology. It's evident in the way we live. We go to God with the big things, but with the little things we tell Him, "No problem, God, I have this one covered. Don't worry about it. I got it."

Jesus said God cares even about the sparrow that falls to the ground.[3] God clothes the lilies of the field.[4] So if God cares about the sparrow and the flower, which are of little significance cosmically and eternally speaking, how much more does He care about you? When Jesus was here on earth, He modeled an altogether different theology than our practical theology. He taught us that the Father is infinitely and intimately concerned with our comings and our goings, with the details of our lives.

A correct view of God is that He is *immanent*, which means working within, and is not to be confused with *imminent*, which means about to happen. The rapture of the Church is imminent. But God is always immanent and working within. Indeed, the Bible teaches that Jesus Christ sustains the world.[5] He's in the midst of our lives. And in that, God prepares us for His purposes. Throughout history, God has chosen to work through people, not independent of people. If God has you waiting, it's because He's working. He works *in you* that He might work *through you*.

---

3. See Matthew 10:29.
4. See Matthew 6:28-30.
5. See Colossians 1:17; Hebrews 1:3.

My Seven Years of Waiting

I mentioned previously that before starting full-time in the ministry, I worked in the family surfboard business. I shaped surfboards and did other things at Channel Islands Surfboards. When I completed my work there, I would minister. There was a period of seven years where I didn't know which one God would ultimately call me into full-time. I knew I couldn't do both for the rest of my life. The hours took a toll. For that period of time, I waited on God, knowing there would ultimately be an either/or. I just had that sense.

Both the surfboard business and the ministry appeared to be on a trajectory toward becoming full-time work. Actually, they were both already full-time, so I guess I was working double-time. Trying to do both was going to totally consume my life and the life of my family. It was unsustainable. I knew God was leading me to one or the other, but for seven years I waited.

During my wait, I taught and preached the Word of God, shaped surfboards and shared the gospel with my co-workers. God told me this: "You be faithful with what I've given you now." So when He had me teaching the Bible, my job was to be faithful with that. When He had me shaping surfboards, my job was to be faithful with that. And in the midst of that surfboard factory, my job was to represent Jesus Christ to the nonbelievers there. It's interesting that it took me about seven years to share the gospel with everyone in that factory—not because there were so many, but because I was so scared. Once I had shared the gospel with everyone there, God called me into full-time, vocational ministry and told me to put the surfboard thing on the altar.

Those seven years of waiting were active, not passive. I didn't just sit back; I pressed in. In that time, God shaped me. When I thought I was shaping surfboards, God was shaping me. See, when you're shaping surfboards, you're all alone. And I'd shape surfboards for anywhere from three to ten hours a day, depending on the day. You're just alone in this little blue room. It gets really weird. One of the cool things about it was I could play sermon tapes and worship music all the time.

That was my seminary, my training. I listened to thousands of sermons and Bible teachings in that little eight-foot by twelve-foot room. When I listened to worship music, I'd often shut the door and end up on my knees in the foam dust, weeping before the Lord—for no reason other than He was with me. I found Him in that little room, and while I was waiting, God was working. At the right moment, and not a moment before, He called me to that purpose that He had for me. But the protocol of waiting on God is to be active and not passive.

Waiting Without Causing Problems

In Genesis 16, the story of Abraham and Sarah takes a major twist as they begin to get impatient in their waiting. It's one thing to be active while waiting; it's another to take things into your own hands and take over for God. Watch what happens in the first two verses:

> Now Sarai, Abram's wife had borne him no children, and she had an Egyptian maid whose name was Hagar. So Sarai said to Abram, "Now behold, the LORD has prevented me from bearing children. Please go in to my maid; perhaps I will obtain children through her." And Abram listened to the voice of Sarai.

If you're a married man, do NOT listen to your wife if she ever says something like that. This is the one time where you totally don't listen to her. Abraham listened to his wife, had sexual relations with Hagar, and then we read in verses 15-16:

> So Hagar bore Abram a son; and Abram called the name of his son, whom Hagar bore, Ishmael. Abram was eighty-six years old when Hagar bore Ishmael to him.

When Abraham was 75 and Sarah was 65, they believed God. But 10 years later, they didn't. They decided to help God. Ishmael became the proverbial work of the flesh—probably the most noteworthy instance in the Bible of God's people taking God's promises into their own hands. Ishmael caused a lot of problems, in Abraham's life and in the life of his offspring for generations to come.

This act of taking the situation into their hands was simply a lack of trust. We all have a propensity to do this, don't we?

Surrender

One day during a visit with my friend Bo, I asked, "What's so hard about waiting on God?" And immediately he said, "Surrender. Surrender is really hard. I've got to surrender my desires, my wisdom. I've got to trust the Lord with everything. I have to trust that the Lord is smarter than me. I've got to surrender the desire to be comfortable. I have to surrender this desire to know the plan. I know God's gonna get me to point B, but I want to know what's between point A and point B. I've got to surrender that continually. And one of the hardest things I have to surrender is my desire to be the provider for my family. I'm not providing for my wife or for my two kids anymore. I'm having to trust God to do that." And that can be hard on a man.

It's even more difficult because we don't have a society or even a Christian culture that values waiting. Most people value "just doing it" and "gittin'r done." Waiting created relational difficulties for Bo, because people looked at him, saying, "What are you doing? Do something!" He felt judged, and he also struggled with doubt because his actions didn't make sense to a lot of people.

"But the hardest thing," Bo said, "is this: I feel like I could fix the problem. I mean I really could. I could make a few phone calls and it would be over. But God isn't letting me."

I said, "Good job, brother. Good job obeying God and not birthing an Ishmael." There's usually something we can do to try to fix the problem. It's not always true in life, but there are many times that we can create a solution ourselves. But that would be birthing an Ishmael.

We need to learn to wait without causing problems, and the works of the flesh always cause problems.

Waiting Without Missing God's Promises

Abraham and Sarah received an incredible promise—something so amazing to them that they could hardly believe it. In Genesis 18:11-15, we see Sarah almost miss the promise of God:

> Now Abraham and Sarah were old, advanced in age; Sarah was past childbearing. Sarah laughed to herself, saying, "After I have become old, shall I have pleasure, my lord being old also?" And the LORD said to Abraham, "Why did Sarah laugh, saying, 'Shall I indeed bear a child, when I am so old?' Is anything too difficult for the LORD? At the appointed time I will return to you, at this time next year, and Sarah will have a son." Sarah denied it however, saying, "I did not laugh"; for she was afraid. And He said, "No, but you did laugh."

God made a promise and Sarah was in real danger of missing it. We see the fulfillment of this promise in Genesis 21:1-5:

> Then the LORD took note of Sarah as He had said, and the LORD did for Sarah as He had promised. So Sarah conceived and bore a son to Abraham in his old age, at the appointed time of which God had spoken to him. Abraham called the name of his son who was born to him, whom Sarah bore to him, Isaac. Then Abraham circumcised his son Isaac when he was eight days old, as God had commanded him. Now Abraham was one hundred years old when his son Isaac was born to him.

It's 25 years after they first received the promise. Abraham is now 100 years old and his wife is 90. God made absolutely sure that they could not conceive on their own before He made it happen. God just didn't want them to miss His promises. They knew that it was humanly impossible. But it says in Hebrews 11:12 that Sarah considered Him who promised faithful. She chose to believe. There's the issue. Do you trust God or not? Maybe you don't. And depending on what has happened in your life, that may be very understandable. I have found that when I have trouble with trusting God, I need to return to His story to be reminded of His trustworthiness. Reading the Bible regularly will help you see that God is faithful. It will help to give you the faith required to wait without missing God's promises.

Faith and Reason

Now, when we choose to have faith it doesn't mean that we ignore the facts, though that's a popular misconception. Faith and facts are not mutually exclusive. They can exist side by side. They can occur at the same time. It's not a logical impossibility for both to be true. In fact, they need each other. Faith without reason is called *fideism*. It's the idea that knowledge depends solely on faith or revelation. It's faith without any reason, without any observation. Reason without faith is called *rationalism*. It's the belief that opinions and actions should be based purely on reason and knowledge and not any religious belief or revelation. But faith doesn't mean that we throw away reason, and reason doesn't demand that we throw away faith. Biblical faith is a composite of the two.

Abraham and Sarah did not take an unreasonable leap of faith. As R. Kent Hughes says, "They weighed the human impossibility of becoming parents against the divine impossibility of God being able to break His Word and decided that since God is God, nothing is impossible."[6] They believed when God said in Genesis 18:14, "Is anything too difficult for the LORD?" They didn't know how God would do it, but they believed that He would.

---

6. Kent Hughes, *Preaching the Word: Hebrews,* vol. 2 (Wheaton, IL: Crossway Books, 1993), p. 100.

The key is not to engage in faith without reason (fideism), or reason without faith (rationalism). Again, R. Kent Hughes explains, "We are to rationally assess all of life. We are to live reasonably. When we are aware that God's Word says thus and so, we are to rationally assess it. Does God's Word actually say that or is it man's fallible interpretation? And if God's Word does indeed say it, then we must be supremely rational, weighing the human impossibility against the divine impossibility of God being able to break His Word. And we must believe."[7]

In other words, what is most rational is to take God at His Word. It is more reasonable than trusting our circumstances or even empirical data. The most reasonable thing possible is to trust God, who has proven Himself trustworthy. That's why the psalmist said in Psalm 130:5: "I wait for the LORD, and my soul does wait, and in His word do I hope." It all depends on what you see as reasonable.

---

7. Kent Hughes, *Preaching the Word: Hebrews,* vol. 2, p. 100.

8

FAITH WELL-TRIED

Abraham with Isaac

By faith Abraham, when he was tested, offered up Isaac, and he who had received the promises was offering up his only begotten son; it was he to whom it was said, "In Isaac your descendants shall be called." He considered that God is able to raise people even from the dead, from which he also received him back as a type.

HEBREWS 11:17-19

IF YOU'VE EVER WONDERED why Abraham is looked to as the father of faith, the father of the faithful and perhaps the greatest example of faith throughout the Bible, this story will make it clear. That one little line—the first part of Hebrews 11:17—says it all: "By faith Abraham, when he was tested, offered up Isaac." This story will show us a faith well-tried, faith tested to the limits and ultimately proven. Now Abraham had already been tried and tested by God when called to leave his home and journey to an unknown land. He had been tested and well-tried when he waited for 25 years on the promise of God for the birth of his son, Isaac. But this would be the greatest test of all. Abraham's faith would be tried, tested and stretched beyond imagination. Genesis 22 gives us the full story of what went down, starting with the first two verses:

> Now it came about after these things, that God tested Abraham, and said to him, "Abraham!" And he said, "Here I am." He said, "Take now your son, your only son, whom you love, Isaac, and go to the land of Moriah, and offer him there as a burnt offering on one of the mountains of which I will tell you."

As we look at this historical event, we need to realize that human sacrifice was not beyond the range of Abraham's experience. Historically speaking, human sacrifice was practiced in Ur, his former home, and in the native culture of Canaan, his current home. So it wasn't really inconceivable that God might ask Abraham to do this. Remember, this was before the Law, before Sinai, before the Torah, and before the Old Testament. As an ancient Middle Easterner, Abraham also realized what a burnt offering meant. First he would have to cut the offering's throat, then dismember it, and then finally all the body parts would be offered up in the fire and consumed by the flames, there on the altar.

This is the horror that Abraham faced. He had been asked to do that to his promised son and miracle child, Isaac. You might wonder how God could be so cruel. But step back a moment and consider this: Has not God Himself done the same? Did not God give His only begotten Son for you and me, and for every sinner? And should not God teach us the value of willingly giving something up that is precious to us for righteousness' sake? Should not God teach us this, even if the lesson comes vicariously through the patriarchs? If we're to understand the cross, humanity must lay hold of the reality of what it means to sacrifice something that we consider immeasurably precious for the sake of righteousness.

Still, we are repulsed that God would ask Abraham to sacrifice his only begotten son. Why? Because we have an anthropocentric worldview and theology. We are horribly and completely man-centered in our fallenness. Somehow, in our perverted psyches, we value Isaac and our own sons above the Son of God. We are terribly anthropocentric in our worldview and in our theology, aren't we? We need to repent of this. When we look at what God asked of Abraham, we need to remember that God did the same with one who was far more precious than a million Isaacs: Jesus Christ.

With that understanding, read Genesis 22:1-2 again:

> Now it came about after these things, that God tested Abraham, and said to him, "Abraham!" And he said, "Here I am." He said, "Take now your son, your only son, whom you love, Isaac, and go to the land of Moriah, and offer him there as a burnt offering on one of the mountains of which I will tell you."

The Purpose of Testing

In both Genesis 22:1 and Hebrews 11:17, it says that God tested Abraham. But what does that mean? Why would God test Abraham? And does God still do that today? Might you or I expect to be tested by God? To answer these questions, let's first examine the idea of testing. Testing has to do with faith. God tested Abraham purposefully to strengthen and build his faith, in order for faith to grow. For faith to be strengthened and built, it must be exercised. Think about your body for a moment. If our muscles are to get stronger and grow, we need to exercise them, right? We all know this, though very few do it. Our muscles don't grow and are not quite right unless we exercise. (Now, there are those anomalies, those people that just naturally have a six-pack and the triceps and the biceps without any effort, and I hate them. I've done a million sit-ups in my life, and still I have nothing but flab and flub, wiggle and jiggle. If you're one of those people who are just naturally cut, I say this in love: we all hate you.)

Like that person who has a God-given six-pack, there are people who have a supernatural endowment of faith—the gift of faith—something that's not necessarily exercised and built up, but just given. That's not the norm. For most of us, faith needs to be exercised, just as our bodies need to be exercised to be functioning at their best. This was true even for Abraham. Though his faith was already tremendous, God tested Abraham in order to exercise his faith.

Testing Is Not Tempting

It's important to realize that testing and tempting are not the same, and that God does not tempt people. James 1:13-14 states this explicitly:

> Let no one say when he is tempted, "I am being tempted by God"; for God cannot be tempted by evil, and He Himself does not tempt anyone. But each one is tempted when he is carried away and enticed by his own lust.

So there's a difference between temptation and testing. The enemy designs *temptation* for our failure, but God designs *testing* for our growth. Temptation presents us with an opportunity to mess up. But testing allows for our strengthening and the building up of our faith. Temptation is from Satan, but testing comes from God. Fruit and blessings come from testing.

The Benefits of Passing the Test

Look at James 1:12, the previous verse. It says:

> Blessed is a man who perseveres under trial[1]; for once he has
> been approved, he will receive the crown of life which the Lord
> has promised to those who love Him.

In that verse, the word "approved" could also be translated "passed
the test." When we have withstood the test, there is the promised state
of being blessed. And "blessed" very simply could be translated as
"happy." Happy is the person who perseveres and passes the test, because that testing will yield a good thing. It will bring that person
closer to Jesus Christ, and yield happiness, blessedness in daily life.

James 1:12 also promises that those who pass the test will "receive
the crown of life." In the New Testament a total of five crowns are
promised as rewards to believers. This is one of those five crowns. The
crown of life refers not only to eternal life, but also to the quality of life
we experience here and now.

James 1:2 says, "Consider it all joy, my brethren, when you encounter various trials." Joy when we encounter trials? That's counterintuitive—like so many things in the Christian faith. James continues in
verses 3-4, showing us the benefits of being tested and passing the test:

> Knowing that the testing of your faith produces endurance [or
> steadfastness or patience]. And let endurance have its perfect
> result, so that you may be perfect [meaning mature] and com-
> plete, lacking in nothing.

These are benefits that help us now, in this lifetime. Testing yields
endurance, or patience, or steadfastness, the old-school word. You've

---

1. The *NASB*, as shown here, is correct in saying "under trial" as opposed to the *KJV* and *NKJV*,
which say "temptation." See the Greek πειρασμός (*peirasmos*, Strong's #3986); *temptation(s)*:
a putting to the test, proof, trial; also, in a bad sense, temptation (this specific meaning oc-
curs only in 1 Peter 4:12).

heard that old saying the world uses: *Be careful what you pray for, because you just might get it.* The world thinks, *If you pray for patience, God will give you hard times so you can learn to be patient.* Even though that's just folk theology, I think there's a little bit of truth in it. God develops patience in us through trials, and there just don't seem to be any shortcuts. That's because patience is part of the fruit of the Spirit, as listed in Galatians 5:22-23: "But the fruit of the Spirit is love, joy, peace, patience, kindness, goodness, faithfulness, self-control."

As we spend intimate, meaningful, relational time with the person of Jesus Christ, these things are worked in and through our lives. And we're told expressly that patience, endurance, steadfastness—this fruit of the Spirit—come to us through trial and yields maturity. We will lack nothing and attain maturity in our faith as James 1:4 tells us. And so because of that, the second verse says to consider it all joy. And again, that's counterintuitive. There's nobody that hits a really hard time in life and says, "Oh, awesome! Praise the Lord! This is great! Everything's falling apart. I love it all. This is killer! Yes!" Nobody says that.

We're not called to rejoice in the fact of the *trial*. That's just masochism. We're called to rejoice in the *results* that are worked in our life by the Holy Spirit of God. But because we as the Church live as an eschatological community—a community that lives in the here and now, but with future truths and realities in mind—we rejoice in the present moment according to a future hope. That's how faith works. Faith has a future hope—it is the assurance of things hoped for, the conviction of things not seen, Hebrews 11:1 says. And so we're not rejoicing in the difficulty, but we *are* rejoicing that we have a God who will work all things together for good for those who love Him and are called according to His purpose.[2] And therefore, we submit ourselves willfully, joyfully and expectantly to the testing of God because of the promised outcome. As Paul says in Romans 5:3-5:

---

2. See Romans 8:28.

We can rejoice, too, when we run into problems and trials, for we know that they help us develop endurance. And endurance develops strength of character, and character strengthens our confident hope of salvation. And this hope will not lead to disappointment. For we know how dearly God loves us, because he has given us the Holy Spirit to fill our hearts with his love (*NLT*).

Is It His Plan or My Mess?

We can begin to understand that, according to Scripture, there is tremendous value in certain trials—those trials that are allowed in our lives by God. And we who are "big-Godders"[3] would say that nothing comes into our lives unless God allows it. So when we see that He's allowing trials in our lives, we believe that there must be a purpose, and we submit to His plan. But it's important to draw a distinction between His plans and our messes. We often make messes with our own sin and say, "Oh, God is testing me." If that's the case, He's not testing you. You've misunderstood a teaching at some point. There's a big difference between His plans and our messes, and it's essential to realize that, because if I'm just an idiot who has made a mess, I need to approach God and ask for grace in an entirely different way. It's a different outworking of faith. If I've made a mess, I must come to God in repentance, having faith that He will repair and restore. I must come to God, saying, "Open up a door of hope in the valley of trouble for me, Lord."[4]

On the other hand, if God is testing me, there is usually some meaningful faith action I must take that will exercise and grow me. The disciples experienced this in Matthew 14:22, where it says that Jesus "made the disciples get into the boat and go ahead of Him to the

---

3. "Big Godders" are people who believe in the absolute sovereignty of God and have submitted themselves to His will and His purposes.
4. See Hosea 2:15.

other side." Jesus literally *commanded* them to action, with a military sort of word—*anankazo* in the Greek. I imagine they might have asked, "Jesus, are You coming with us?" And He probably would have replied, "No, boys, you're on your own on this one." So they go out on the water and here comes the sovereignly designed storm. The disciples had never *once* worshiped Jesus Christ until after they had been through that storm.[5] They had seen many miracles, but it wasn't until they had been through a great trial that they worshiped Him and saw Him as the Son of God and God in the flesh. We cannot miss the profundity of that. Trials change hearts.

Better than Gold

There's tremendous value in our faith being tested. First Peter 1:7 highlights this again:

> These trials will show that your faith is genuine. It is being tested as fire tests and purifies gold—though your faith is far more precious than mere gold. So when your faith remains strong through many trials, it will bring you much praise and glory and honor on the day when Jesus Christ is revealed to the whole world (*NLT*).

We want our faith to be genuine and authentic. We want our lives of faith to be strong. And the Bible is clear that this only happens through many trials. God, in His wisdom and in His love, allows certain trials into our lives, and undergoing these trials yields a faith that is more precious in this lifetime than pure, refined gold. Very few of us have really laid hold of that idea—that authentic, genuine, well-tried faith will get us further *in this life* than pure gold. The righteous shall live by faith, and our faith is made genuine and strong through the

---

5. See Matthew 14:32-33.

process of testing. Without testing, we don't have the opportunities to succeed and therefore to grow. Testing forces us to make faith decisions. It makes us respond to circumstances according to the wisdom of God, the Word of God, the ways of God and the grace of God. It forces us to take meaningful faith action. That's how testing exercises us and sets us up for success, not failure.

One Step at a Time

It's important to realize that Abraham's test came *after* substantial spiritual growth and blessing. God worked in Abraham's life the same way He works in our lives—progressively. He doesn't do it all at once. Can you imagine if God revealed all your sin to you all at one time? You would freak out. But God is kind. He reveals just enough so you'll come to Him and repent, "Jesus, help me! Be my Lord and Savior!" And then some time later, you're like, "Cool, I'm all good now." And then He says, "Well, actually . . . look at this." And He shows us a little bit more of our sin, and it gets us back on our face. This is a nonstop process, God showing us our sins a little at a time. He's good like that.

Not only does He do that with our sin, but He also works progressively with our faith. Like a kind father, He leads us with baby steps. Even with Abraham, though they were big steps—he was Abraham, after all—it was still a progressive process. It was "leave your home and family, leave that place where you're from, go to a land that I'll show you and dwell there. Wait for the promised son." Only *then* did He say, "Now give your son as a sacrifice." God was good to do it progressively. He was building faith into Abraham's life. And the good things that God had already done, the faith lessons that Abraham had already learned, set the groundwork for greater testing and greater growth.

What really did it for Abraham was the process of waiting on God. Abraham waited on God for 25 years. Yes, he had some failures and follies in that time, but nonetheless he waited on God. And even though none of us like to wait, because waiting feels like work, when we're waiting on God, there's a work that is accomplished in our lives. He purges things out of our hearts that shouldn't be there. He fortifies or builds into our lives things that *should* be there. And I would suggest to you that only because Abraham had been through the process of waiting on God, and submitted himself to the resulting work of God, was he ready to be well-tested.

What About Me?

God put Abraham through a difficult trial for a simple reason: to develop in him greater faith, greater character and greater hope, to the glory of God. Does God still do that today? Absolutely. Can you expect God to do something like this in your life? You'd better count on it. There's no question about it. If God loves you, He will do these things in your life. And God *does* love you, so He *will* test you. He may be testing you right now. The problem is, we often fail to recognize the testing.

If you're anything like me, you are pretty much totally self-absorbed. You get caught up in yourself and your own drama—how you feel, the stuff you want, your daily goings-on, your fun things—and sometimes miss what God is trying to do. It might be that we fall back on our own ingenuity when we experience a trial. We birth an Ishmael and think we've gotten around it for a little while. Or we just insulate ourselves from those difficult things by not dealing with them. We cut off relationships that God would want to use to refine us, keeping ourselves from accountability. We think these actions will protect us, but instead they just cause us to miss the fact that God might be testing us for His own good and His own glory. Sometimes it's not that we *miss* them; it's that we *misname* them. We make our own messes and then call them tests. It's crucial for us to discern between a mess we made and a test from God.

We can learn from both the faith and the testing of Abraham that God *will sometimes test us in regard to what we value highly to make sure that we value Him most.* He's going to go right for the thing that you value the most. He went right for the son that Abraham had waited on for so long. And though Abraham's faith was radically tested, he came out successful.

Why Abraham Passed the Test

Abraham passed the test because of three simple reasons:

1. Abraham was convinced about God's goodness.
2. Abraham was convinced about God's plan.
3. Abraham was convinced about God's power.

In Genesis 22, we see how these three reasons play out. First, Abraham was convinced about God's goodness. He firmly believed in it, and that made him able to do what God called him to do. Beyond what he could see, beyond even what he could understand, he trusted that God was good. He really believed it. It wasn't a rote confession for him. It wasn't a cute little Christian stadium cheer—"God is good, all the time, all the time, God is good." It was *real* for him. He firmly believed that God was good and that enabled him to do the extremely difficult things that God called him to do. Wouldn't you like to have faith like that?

The Tasty Goodness of God

We all want to become as convinced of God's goodness as Abraham was. But how? I'll share with you one of the ways that have worked in my life.

When I was shaping surfboards for 12 years or so, I had some verses up in my shaping room. Among the most prominently displayed was Psalm 34:8: "O taste and see that the LORD is good; how blessed is the man who takes refuge in Him!" It hung up there for over a decade. I looked at it almost every single day and it radically affected my life. It became a pivotal, formational verse for me. *Taste and see that the Lord is good.* If we're going to be honest, empirical realities—that which can be tested, looked at, and handled—those things don't always speak to us of the goodness of God. As we look around the world, so much of what we see causes us to think, *God is good? Really? Can that be true?* And yet the psalmist beckons us, saying, "Well why don't you taste and see? Quit asking and start tasting."

If you want to taste something, you have to experience it. So if you want to "taste and see that the Lord is good," get involved with God. Begin to handle the Word of God and experience the things of God. I mean, really get involved—commingle your life with the life of Christ. Cultivate an intimate, meaningful love relationship with Him, and you'll begin to experience Him. You'll begin to taste Him. And when you do, you will find that He is good. You'll *see* that He is good. And you'll also discover His goodness is *beyond* what you can or can't see.

Remember that the righteous are called to walk by faith and not by sight.[6] While we're called to see that the Lord is good, sometimes that means looking beyond the immediately visible. So in your own life now, if you want to develop a deep conviction—like Abraham—that God is good, look for ways to experience God. Probably your best opportunity to do that is to open your Bible every day. We also experience God in prayer and worship and by obeying Him. That's how we experience the reality of the Gospels—we obey God's call to repent. The first word that Jesus ever said in His public ministry was "repent."[7] When we obey that command, we experience the goodness of God and the grace of God and the forgiveness of God through the cross of Jesus Christ and His resurrection from the dead. But if we had never obeyed the command to repent, we never would have known that God was good.

---

6. See 2 Corinthians 5:7.
7. See Matthew 4:17.

The opposite is also true: The *less* you obey God, the *less* you will experience that God is good. You may have an ethereal theological understanding. *Oh, God is good. I'm forgiven for that again.* But you'll never really lay hold of it and be convinced of it. If you want to taste and see that the Lord is good, there is no better way than to obey Him in the minutiae of your life as the Holy Spirit seeks to refine you.

Obeying Immediately

Abraham was convinced of the goodness of God and it made him willing to obey God immediately. This is a biggie. He obeyed *immediately* because he was so convinced of God's goodness. Look at Genesis 22:3: "So Abraham rose early in the morning and saddled his donkey, and took two of his young men with him and Isaac his son; and he split the wood for the burnt offering, and arose and went to the place of which God had told him." Notice that. Abraham got up *early* in the morning. He didn't procrastinate. He didn't say, "Oh, I'll do it later." He was so convinced that God was good, that God's purposes were good and that God would bring good in and through his life that he said: I'm doing this first thing in the morning. As radical as it may seem, he obeyed God immediately.

Here's the problem with us. We often believe that God is *good*, but we don't always believe that He's *better* than whatever it is we're being tempted with, or whatever it is we're involved with. Yes, we know God is good, so we want to obey. But we don't actually always believe that God is better and a better payoff, so we don't always obey right away. It's not that we don't want to obey. We do. It's just that we often don't want to obey right away.

Saint Augustine experienced this hundreds and hundreds of years ago when it came to sexual purity. In his book *Confessions*, he says:

As I prayed to God for the gift of chastity, I had even pleaded: "Grant me chastity and self-control, but please not yet." I was afraid that You might hear me immediately and heal me forthwith of the morbid lust which I was more anxious to satisfy than to snuff out.

Have you ever prayed a prayer like that? I mean, Augustine believed that God was good. He thought, *Yeah, God is good and it'd be good for me to not be sexually immoral and to get over this lust thing,* but he didn't necessarily think that God was better than the payoff of lust. *Not now, God. I want to obey, but can't we wait until a little bit later?* We do that all the time, don't we? But Abraham was so convinced that God was not only good but also that He was better that he was willing to obey immediately.

Convinced of God's Plan; Obeying Persistently

Abraham was not only convinced of God's goodness but also of God's plan. Hebrews 11:17-18 shows us this:

> By faith Abraham, when he was tested, offered up Isaac, and he who had received the promises was offering up his only begotten son; it was he to whom it was said, "In Isaac your descendants shall be called."

God had said to Abraham, "I will make you into a great nation, and I will bless you . . . and in you all the families of the earth will be blessed."[8] That's what made Abraham willing to obey persistently. He was convinced of God's *goodness*, so he was willing to obey *immediately*, and he was convinced of God's *plan*, so he was willing to obey *persistently*. Abraham would obey, even in a prolonged situation and when the going got tough. And that's life, isn't it? Things usually take a little longer and are a little more difficult than we think. Genesis 22:4-8 provides an extreme example of this:

8. Genesis 12:2-3.

On the third day Abraham raised his eyes and saw the place from a distance. Abraham said to his young men, "Stay here with the donkey, and I and the lad will go over there; and we will worship and return to you." Abraham took the wood of the burnt offering and laid it on Isaac his son, and he took in his hand the fire and the knife. So the two of them walked on together. Isaac spoke to Abraham his father and said, "My father!" And he said, "Here I am, my son." And he said, "Behold, the fire and the wood, but where is the lamb for the burnt offering?" Abraham said, "God will provide for Himself the lamb for the burnt offering, my son." So the two of them walked on together.

Things were getting really difficult for Abraham right about now, in every possible way. He got up early in the morning to obey God. But now that he was in the thick of it, he had to continue to obey. He had to obey persistently. To do this, he had to be really convinced of God's plan, because it was getting hard. Imagine his situation. He's been journeying for three days, and now he comes to the area of Mt. Moriah, which incidentally is the same bedrock section in Jerusalem where Christ was crucified and where the Temple Mount is located. He gets there and now he's got to offload the wood from the donkey to get up the hill and put it on Isaac. Because he took the wood off the donkey and put it on Isaac, we can only assume that the hill was too steep for the donkey to go up. And he also has to carry up the fire. I don't know what that meant 4,000 years ago, but it was probably some drama. I mean he's got some fire and he's got to take it with him. It probably just wasn't like some lighter fluid and a Bic. Getting this whole fire gig going back then might have been a little difficult. And his son is carrying the wood, and he starts questioning his father: "Dad, where is the lamb?"

It must have been getting really hard for Abraham to follow through with what he knew God had called him to do. Right now he needed perseverance and persistence in his obedience, and the only thing that allowed him to persevere was that he was *absolutely convinced of God's plan*. He really believed that God would make a great nation come forth from Isaac. He really believed that God would bless the nations with a Messiah, through his descendants. He really believed God's plan, and therefore was fully committed to it.

Are You All In?

We need to ask ourselves as Christians if we are committed fully to God's plan—His macro plan as it pertains to the nations *and* his micro plan for your life. Are you committed fully to the plan of God? If you are, then you're going to persevere in your obedience. When things are difficult, you'll make it through by the grace of God for the glory of God. And that's what had to happen in Abraham's life.

During the seven years that I worked both in the family surfboard business and doing ministry, I thought I was just shaping surfboards. But as I mentioned before, I came to realize that it was *God* who was shaping *me* during those years—convincing me that His plan was better. I had a plan to shape surfboards and to eventually take over the business. And my parents had the same plan. There was nothing in the world I wanted to be more than a surfboard shaper. I loved it. I dreamed about surfboards; I thought about surfboards; I rode surfboards; I made surfboards; I ate, slept and drank surfboards. I loved that life and was so thankful to God that would be my life. But at some point I discovered that God had a different plan, and this was just a stop along the way. And for seven years after that, I waited on God—because both the ministry and surfboard shaping were on a trajectory such that both of them could not simultaneously exist forever. There were just too many demands.

I knew in my heart that it would have to be one or the other. And for seven years, though I didn't fully realize it, God worked in my heart to convict me and convince me that His plan was better—better than anything I thought possible. I didn't think there could be a better gig than taking over Channel Islands Surfboards. But God convinced me in my intimate quiet times with Him, on my face before Him, that His plan was better.

At first, I didn't have great faith, but I tried, by grace, to obey. And when God gave me little things to do—like leading a Bible study with six kids, or making a surfboard for a great surfer—I would try to be diligent with them. I would be consistent in showing up and being there for the kids. I'd put my all into making the surfboard and then share the gospel with that surfer. Whatever God gave me to do, I tried to be faithful doing it. And as I did, I not only discovered God's plan, but I also discovered that God's plan is better. We discover God's plan—and realize that it's better—when we choose to live it. Be faithful in the little things that God calls you to do. You'll find that he who is faithful with little will be entrusted with more.[9]

Convinced of God's Power; Obeying Ultimately

Not only was Abraham convinced of God's goodness and His plan, but he was also convinced of God's power. That is what ultimately made him willing to obey. He obeyed immediately, he obeyed continually and he obeyed ultimately, as shown in Genesis 22:9-18:

> Then they came to the place of which God had told him; and Abraham built the altar there and arranged the wood, and bound his son Isaac and laid him on the altar, on top of the wood.
>
> Abraham stretched out his hand and took the knife to slay his son. But the angel of the LORD called to him from heaven and said, "Abraham, Abraham!" And he said, "Here I am."
>
> He said, "Do not stretch out your hand against the lad, and do nothing to him; for now I know that you fear God, since you have not withheld your son, your only son, from Me."

---

9. See Luke 16:10.

Then Abraham raised his eyes and looked, and behold, behind him a ram caught in the thicket by his horns; and Abraham went and took the ram and offered him up for a burnt offering in the place of his son.

Abraham called the name of that place The LORD Will Provide, [Jehovah Jireh] as it is said to this day, "In the mount of the LORD it will be provided."[10]

Then the angel of the LORD called to Abraham a second time from heaven, and said, "By Myself I have sworn, declares the LORD, because you have done this thing and have not withheld your son, your only son, indeed I will greatly bless you, and I will greatly multiply your seed as the stars of the heavens and as the sand which is on the seashore; and your seed shall possess the gate of their enemies. In your seed all the nations of the earth shall be blessed, because you have obeyed My voice."

Wow, what a promise! The promise of the Messiah, the ram caught in the thicket, foreshadowing Jesus, the Lamb of God who died for the sins of the world. And these giant things, to some degree, were dependent upon the obedience of this *one man* thousands of years ago. You just never know what God is going to do. Abraham had to obey God ultimately. And notice the past tense in verse 16. God said, "Because you *have done* this thing," even though Abraham never actually slit the throat of Isaac. Abraham would have, though. In his heart it was settled. He was ready to follow through on the thing that God called him to do. But God stopped him. And in stopping him, God revealed to Abraham that He was not like the gods of the Canaanites. Essentially, God said, "I will not ask from you a human sacrifice, but I Myself will be draped in humanity and be sacrificed for you. I am different from

---

10. This is a foreshadowing of Christ, as Jesus would be crucified on that very same piece of bedrock in Jerusalem, Mount Moriah.

the gods of the land. I am a God who gives. But now you understand to what extent I will give. I will give My only begotten Son."

Abraham Did It

Hebrews 11:17 confirms that in the mind of God, Abraham went all the way. It says, "By faith Abraham, when he was tested, offered up Isaac." "Offered up" is in the perfect tense in the Greek. It means it was a completed, past action with present results. In the mind of God, it was done! Abraham offered up Isaac. Meaning he gave Isaac, or surrendered him. So not only was this act done, but it had *present results*—the blessing in his life and the blessing among the nations. Abraham made it. He passed the test when he obeyed immediately, continually and ultimately.

We also read in 11:19 that Abraham considered that God is able to raise people from the dead. Genesis 22:5 gives further proof of this: "Abraham said to his young men, 'Stay here with the donkey, and I and the lad will go over there; and we will worship and return to you.'" Abraham said, "We will return to you," showing his confidence of coming back down Mount Moriah with Isaac. He was so convinced of God's plan that it forced him to rely upon God's power. The doctrine of resurrection had not yet been given to man, but by faith and by reason—because he believed God was good and he was convinced of God's plan—he knew that God must have the power to raise men even from the dead. After all, Abraham was as good as dead at 100 years old when Isaac was conceived. And now, as he went up the mountain, he thought he would burn his son on the altar and then God would resurrect him from the ashes. And in essence, he was right! He understood the doctrine of the resurrection before it had been revealed to anyone else in humanity. Abraham's faith was incredible.

Done in Worship

When Genesis 22:5 says "we will go and worship," it's the first time in the Bible the word "worship" is used. This most pivotal moment in

Abraham's life came in the context of worship. It's important to recognize that some of the most important moments of clarity and profundity in our lives come when we worship.

I love what Abraham said in Genesis 22:8, when asked by Isaac, "Where is the lamb?" Abraham responded, "God will provide for Himself the lamb." In saying that, he was really saying, "Son, I trust God implicitly." He trusted without qualification. But he left room for God to be God. He didn't know *how* God was going to do it. He just knew that God would! And he said, "I trust God. I'm not leaning on my own understanding. I don't have the play-by-play. I don't have the moment-by-moment. But I've got the plan, I know the goodness of God and I understand the power of God, so I trust God without reservation. I don't know how He's going to do it, but He's God. That's His problem!" He saw this situation as God's problem and not his own—and that's one of the benefits of obeying. When you obey, the outcome is God's problem. If God called you to do it, God will handle it. Abraham figured that if God was going to make a multitude of descendants come from Isaac, God was just going to have to resurrect him from the dead!

God Is Able

We see Abraham's attitude in Hebrews 11:19: "He considered that God is able." The word "considered" here is *logizomai* in the Greek. It's the same root word from which we get our word "logic." Abraham "considered," meaning he reckoned, calculated, reasoned, thought. This was not blind faith, nor fideism—faith apart from reason. Nor was this rationalism—reason without faith. This was biblical faith—a conglomeration of faith and reason. Abraham made a reasoned, reckoned, calculated decision based on what he knew about God—God's character, God's plan and God's power. And he said, "It makes more sense that God would raise my son from the dead than that He would go back on His promise." That's faith! It wasn't blind. It wasn't stupid. It wasn't mindless. Abraham believed the power of God was bigger than the circumstances he faced. Abraham was a "big-Godder." Faith means being sure of things we hope for and knowing that something is real even if we do not see it.

Abraham passed the test. And so he goes down on record as a friend of God. James 2:21-23 says:

> Was not Abraham our father justified by works when he offered up Isaac his son on the altar? You see that faith was working with his works, and as a result of the works, faith was perfected; and the Scripture was fulfilled which says, "And Abraham believed God, and it was reckoned to him as righteousness," and he was called the friend of God.

Who Do You Love?

In my own life I wanted nothing more in the world than to be a surfboard shaper. I valued that highly. In 1998 God put His hand on that. Yes, it took seven years for me to be convinced of God's plan, that it was better. But there was a day—I will never forget it—when I said, "Lord, I put it on the altar." Like Abraham, I put my Isaac on the altar: my own hopes, my own dreams, the things that I love, my identity, everything I ever wanted to do. "God," I said, "I put it on the altar, because I'm convinced that You're good, that You're better. I'm convinced that Your plan is better. And I'm convinced of Your power, that You are able."

After Jesus was resurrected, He said to Peter, "Do you love Me more than these?"[11] The Bible doesn't tell us what "these" are. It might have been the other disciples, or it might have been the boats, the nets, his fishing equipment, his family business. The fact is, it really doesn't matter what "these" are. The Lord simply asked him, "Peter, do you love Me more?" Likewise, Elijah confronted Israel on Mount Carmel, saying, "How long will you hesitate between two opinions? If the Lord is God, follow Him."[12] The apostle Paul got it. In his letter to the Philippians, he

---

11. John 21:15.
12. 1 Kings 18:21.

said, "Whatever things were gain to me, those things I have counted as loss for the sake of Christ. More than that, I count all things to be loss in view of the surpassing value of knowing Christ Jesus my Lord, for whom I have suffered the loss of all things, and count them but rubbish so that I may gain Christ."[13]

God might just put His hand on that which you love a lot to make sure that you love Him the most. What is it that you need to offer up by faith? Have you considered that it might be *you*? As Romans 12:1 says, "I urge you, brethren, by the mercies of God, to present your bodies a living and holy sacrifice, acceptable to God, which is your spiritual service of worship." The one that needs to get on the altar and die might just be you.

---

13. Philippians 3:7-8.

9

FAITH WINNING

Moses

*By faith Moses, when he was born, was hidden
for three months by his parents, because they
saw he was a beautiful child; and they were not
afraid of the king's edict. By faith Moses, when
he had grown up, refused to be called the son
of Pharaoh's daughter, choosing rather to endure ill-treatment with the people of God than
to enjoy the passing pleasures of sin, considering
the reproach of Christ greater riches than the
treasures of Egypt; for he was looking to the
reward. By faith he left Egypt, not fearing the
wrath of the king; for he endured, as seeing Him
who is unseen. By faith he kept the Passover
and the sprinkling of the blood, so that he who
destroyed the firstborn would not touch them.
By faith they passed through the Red Sea as
though they were passing through dry land;
and the Egyptians, when they attempted it,
were drowned.*

HEBREWS 11:23-29

IN OUR JOURNEY OF FAITH we have discovered a wonderful progression. Abel taught us about worshiping by faith. Enoch showed us what it means to walk by faith. Noah demonstrated working by faith. Abraham pictured faith that is willing to go and to forego and to witness and to worship. Sarah illustrated waiting by faith. Abraham instructed us concerning faith that is well-tried. And now, we'll see that Moses exemplifies *winning* by faith. When these accumulative effects take place in our lives of faith, then we'll find we have a faith that wins, like Moses did.

Remember, it's all about the object of our faith: the person of Jesus Christ. He's the Alpha and the Omega, the beginning and the end. He's the genesis of all things and the consummation of all things. He is the One who spoke all things into existence and all things exist for His glory. Jesus has already won through His cross and His resurrection. He has already won, He is currently winning, and He will win. Understand this about Jesus.

Also understand that we are His—identified with Him and co-heirs with Him. Because we are His, when and where He wins, we win. We're in Christ in this life of faith. It's no longer we who live but Christ who lives in us. And the life we live, we live by faith unto Him.[1] Where He has victory, we have victory. Where He has overcome, we shall overcome.

In Romans 8:37, Paul says that we are "more than conquerors through Him who loved us" (*NIV*). Moses conquered three things by faith, and in Christ, by faith, we can win in the same areas: *against fear, against the flesh*, and *against the foe* (meaning Satan, in case you're wondering!). How exactly does faith help us to win? Faith means we believe certain things about who Christ is and about what God has said and done. We trust God's purposes, so we don't fear present circumstances. We trust God's promises, so we don't pursue the things of the flesh. And we trust God's power, so we don't allow the foe to rule

---

1. See Galatians 2:20.

over us. We believe, we confess, and we hold on to certain truths that are seen to be better than, more real than, of greater value than other truths that would set themselves up and against these truths of Christ.

We Win Against Fear

God does not want us to live in fear, a favorite tactic of our foe. Satan works through natural agents to create fear in our lives. The spiritual realm always manifests itself in one way or another in the physical realm, yet it's not really the physical that we war against. As Ephesians 6:12 says, we don't war against flesh and blood but against powers and principalities and spiritual forces of wickedness in high places—in the supernatural realm.

The spiritual realities of Jesus Christ manifest themselves in the life of the Church—in you and me together. Likewise, the spiritual realities of Satan and his kingdom also manifest themselves in people. And there is fear that naturally arises when we encounter confrontations with people who might be agents of the foe. In the story of Moses, the king of Egypt was an agent of the foe. He was an enemy of God and of God's people, and he caused fear in the heart of Moses. In the book of Hebrews, Nero, the emperor of Rome, was an evil, destructive force who persecuted God's people. Moses and the recipients of Hebrews feared not only those ruling earthly powers but also the spiritual forces behind them. But while the sense of fear is natural, we aren't to give in to the fear.

Hebrews 11:23 shows us this in the life and faith of Moses' parents, Amram and Jochebed:

By faith Moses, when he was born, was hidden for three months by his parents, because they saw he was a beautiful child; and they were not afraid of the king's edict.

Look at Moses later on in verse 27:

173

By faith he left Egypt, not fearing the wrath of the king; for he endured, as seeing Him who is unseen.

So the background story is necessary for us here. It starts as the book of Genesis closes, with Joseph rising to a position of power in Egypt—second in command to Pharaoh. His family then comes to Egypt and finds a place there, prospering and multiplying. But then Exodus opens with these words a few verses into it: "Now a new king arose over Egypt, who did not know Joseph."[2]

That new king didn't care about Joseph and his previous high standing. And he didn't care about the people of Israel, these foreigners within the land who were prospering. In fact, he saw them as a threat. So the government issued sanctions against Israel in the land of Egypt and made it difficult for them to live there. The king went so far as to order that every male Hebrew child born had to be killed. His goal was to control and contain the increasingly powerful Hebrew population, to prevent the possibility of an uprising or revolution. That should have caused every Hebrew to be filled with fear, right?

Moses Does It His Way

We all know the story of how Moses' parents slid his basket into the river and, after being found later by Pharaoh's daughter, was given back to his own mother to nurse. So Moses was raised in the house of Pharaoh, with all the privileges of the house of Pharaoh—all the riches, all the wealth, all the honor, all the prestige, all the power, all that stuff. Yet Moses knew he was called by God to be the deliverer of Israel. One day he saw an Egyptian guard beating a Hebrew slave and he couldn't take it anymore. Righteous indignation welled up in him as he watched his people suffering violent injustice. So he took it upon himself to kill that Egyptian guard and immediately had to flee. That's what Hebrews

---

2. Exodus 1:8.

11:27 is talking about when it says, "By faith he left Egypt, not fearing the wrath of the king, but he endured, as seeing him who is unseen."

Moses didn't flee because he was afraid of the wrath of the king. Moses fled because he had taken God's purposes into his own hands. He tried to accomplish the work of God his own way, and that never works. You've got to do God's work God's way, and if you do—just like Moses' parents did—you will never lack God's provision.[3] So Moses, by faith, went into the wilderness. But God is good, even when we mess up. Moses met a lady out there, got married, started raising sheep and eventually had that whole burning bush experience.[4] Forty years later, after much humbling, after all the power and prestige and all the reality of being a son of Pharaoh were purged out of him and he was made a shepherd of sheep, God sent him back to shepherd the sheep of Israel with the mighty outstretched hand of God.

It's an incredible story of overcoming fear of perverse world systems. In America we can be thankful that we don't have a system like the one Moses experienced. Yes, it's true that we don't have a perfect government. But as Christians in this nation, we are not under a king who is wanting to kill us or our babies. In other parts of the world, however, people—our brothers and sisters in Christ—live under the reality of a government like that of Pharaoh, or that of Nero, a government that wants to eliminate the people of God. This is a reality in the world, even today.

A Different Sort of Persecution and Pressure

Those of us in America just don't face that kind of persecution. But there is a different sort of pressure that we do face, and it causes fear that is just as real. It's the pressure of opposing religious views. That's a big deal in America. We have religious freedom in America, and that's a

---

3. "God's work done God's way will never lack God's provision" is a quote from Hudson Taylor, the famous missionary to inland China.
4. For the full story of that part of Moses' life, check out Exodus 2:15–3:22.

wonderful thing. But it comes with some real tensions. Islam is growing rapidly in this country,[5] as well as cults and other religions. Perhaps the fastest-growing religion in America is secular humanism. Christianity and secular humanism are on a collision course in this country.

This has been unfolding for some time, and what we see now is that American society is becoming both more religious *and* more secular at the same time. The result is a greater polarization among the population. Ultimately, that brings with it some degree of confrontation, whether it's in the spiritual realm through prayer, or in the physical realm through action or debate. It could be an issue of prayer in schools, or an issue of the expression of the Christian faith in the public forum. Whatever it is, confrontation can arise, and this tends to bring fear among Christians. We feel outnumbered, out-voiced, out-voted.

The disciples in the first century experienced persecution at the hands of the religious Jews, who, in Acts 4, grabbed hold of them, threw them in jail, and said, "You must stop talking about Jesus!" They didn't have any first-amendment right to appeal to. They didn't have *any* rights guaranteed by a constitution. They were told expressly by the powers of the land, "You need to stop talking about Jesus. We're done with this." And Peter looked at them and said, "Whether it is right in the sight of God to give heed to you rather than to God, you be the judge; for we cannot stop speaking about what we have seen and heard."[6]

We know that despite his boldness, fear still gripped Peter. He said in a prayer meeting, "God, make us bold." They wouldn't pray for boldness if there wasn't a lack of it. There was some real, tangible, societal conflict that caused fear in their hearts. And so we read in Acts 4:29-31:

> "And now, Lord, take note of their threats, and grant that Your bond-servants may speak Your word with all confidence, while

---

5. A *New York Times* article from October 22, 2001, titled "Islam Attracts Converts by the Thousands," states: "With some 6 million adherents in the United States, Islam is said to be the nation's fastest-growing religion, fueled by immigration, high birth rates and widespread conversion."

6. Acts 4:19-20.

You extend Your hand to heal, and signs and wonders take place through the name of Your holy servant Jesus." And when they had prayed, the place where they had gathered together was shaken, and they were all filled with the Holy Spirit and began to speak the word of God with boldness.

Note the answer to the problem: prayer and the power of the Holy Spirit. The answer wasn't found in the ballot box, though we should vote, and we should vote righteously. The answer wasn't found in the political forum, though Christians should be involved in politics. The answer was found in a prayer meeting.

Where Is the Power?

We've had Christian presidents in America—and that's the pinnacle of political power. But that's not the source of real power. Real power is in the person of the Holy Spirit, and we access that power in prayer. We come to God and present Him with a spiritual problem that has manifested in the physical realm. Like Peter did, we go to God and say, "God, we need spiritual power to confront this problem." He will give us wisdom and guide us in the best way to overcome the problem. He might lead us into politics, or give us influence in other sectors of society. But we do it in His power, because ultimately these are all spiritual issues that can only be addressed with spiritual means—with the power of the Holy Spirit.

Today, so much of the Church is void of power because so much of the Church is void of prayer. If the Church would pray more, the Church would have more power—not in and of herself, but in the person of the Holy Spirit. We would see more communal, societal change. The battle is won on our knees. One of the greatest marvels in the history of this world is that Christianity started in a little manger in Bethlehem and within 300 years was the official religion of the Roman Empire. Much of that can be attributed to the early Church addressing spiritual problems with spiritual means. They prayed and they relied upon the power of the person of the Holy Spirit. That's a faith decision.

Don't Give In!

By faith we don't give in to fear. We don't live in fear of competing religions and competing ideologies. Instead, we confront them in boldness with love, gentleness and reverence. But we must confront them. We can't back down, because it's the worst kind of hypocrisy to believe that without Jesus Christ people are going to hell and then to stay silent about it.

Moses' parents didn't do that. Moses didn't do that. The early Church didn't do that. In 2 Timothy 1:7-10, Paul says:

> For God has not given us a spirit of timidity, but of power and love and discipline. Therefore do not be ashamed of the testimony of our Lord or of me His prisoner, but join with me in suffering for the gospel according to the power of God, who has saved us and called us with a holy calling, not according to our works, but according to His own purpose and grace which was granted us in Christ Jesus from all eternity, but now has been revealed by the appearing of our Savior Christ Jesus, who abolished death and brought life and immortality to light through the gospel.

When we're struggling with fear, it's not from God. He has not given us a spirit of fear.

Paul said in Romans 1:16, "I am not ashamed of the gospel, for it is the power of God for salvation." To be completely transparent with you, this verse really speaks to me. Because nearly all of us—including me—experience some sort of fear when it comes to representing Jesus Christ in the public forum. There are some who don't—gifted evangelists on the street in fifth gear, just doing it. But normal folks like you and me experience fear in that situation. It's really weird for me because I'll be as bold as a lion in a pulpit. Put me in a pulpit in front of 10,000 people, and I won't sweat that for a minute. I'm ready to go. I don't care how big the crowd is or who they are. But put me in Coffee Bean and Tea Leaf with a friend from high school who says, "So what are you up to these days?" and my immediate, visceral response is fear.

The Fear of Rejection

Often what we really fear is relational rejection. I'm afraid that if I start talking about Jesus, my old friends or new acquaintances will think I'm trying to shove Jesus down their throats and they're not going to want to be my friends. Even worse, they'll think I'm lame and a dork. And so I sit on the truth. That's wrong. I don't want to be that way, but that's what comes out in those situations. But I know that the power of the Holy Spirit can transform me.

God can take fearful people like you and me—people who have normal, everyday relationship rejection issues—and make us bold, to the glory of Jesus Christ. As a result, our friends and our families get saved. Faith wins against fear. When we continue in fear, it arrests our development. Talking about Jesus, teaching about Jesus, sharing, witnessing, and ministering; a real growth process takes place when we do these things. If we inoculate ourselves, wall up our lives so that we never have to do those things, then our development will be stunted. And if you have stunted growth, you will eventually drift away from Jesus.

That's the whole point of the book of Hebrews, which was written to the Hebrew Christians because they feared Nero. They were afraid of losing their property, of losing their positions in society, even of losing their lives. That fear stunted their growth and as a result they drifted away from the faith. And so the author writes to warn them, "Don't drift!"

Overcoming the Fear

Many of us have arrested development because we're all bound up by fear. But that's not God's will for you. You don't have to be a kook on the corner with a sign on your back, shouting at people, but you do need to be a loving, purposeful, understanding Christian who cares enough to articulate the truths of Jesus Christ when people need to hear it. That's the call on every one of us. I know how that call feels. It can seem like a burden! But that's just the result of our own perversion—of our esteeming people above the purposes of God. That's all it is. So deal with it! Have the boldness to ask the Holy Spirit to come upon you so that you would be transformed, that you would receive power to be His witness wherever you are.

We need to overcome fear, because not only will fear arrest our development but it will also keep us from entering into the promises of God. That's exactly what happened in Numbers 13–14 in Kadesh Barnea. God's people were supposed to enter into the Promised Land, but they were afraid because of the giants. Their fear of the societal, cultural confrontation caused them to back down. Consequently, they missed the promises of God. They wandered in the wilderness for 40 years—until the whole generation died off!

Eyes on the Prize

Hebrews 11:27 tells us that Moses "endured, as seeing Him who is unseen." Or as the *New Living Translation* puts it, "He kept right on going because he kept his eyes on the One who is invisible." He kept on going because his eyes were fixed on God. Moses had tenacity—a tenacity that didn't come naturally, but was developed by faith. Moses had this tenacity in the face of opposition because of faith. He kept his eyes on God. Like Moses, we may know that God has a purpose for our lives. But often we make the mistake of getting our eyes on the purpose instead of the One who purposed. We need to keep our eyes on Jesus. Remember, Peter walked on water as long as he kept his eyes on Jesus. But the moment he got his eyes on the wind and the waves, he began to sink into the very circumstances that he was winning over by faith just a moment before.

We need to keep our eyes on Jesus—daily. Daily choosing the right things, being in the Word, praying, and fellowshipping. If I let a few days go by I start to drift. My mind and eyes wander. And there's plenty to get your eyes on in the world around us. So it's truly a battle for the Christian to keep his or her gaze fixed on Jesus Christ. Do whatever it takes. Are there distractions that need to be cut off? Then cut them off! Are there certain devices that need to be unplugged? Then unplug them! Are there certain disciplines that need to be adopted? Then adopt them! Are there certain friends or relationships that need to be surrendered? Then surrender them. Whatever you need to fix your eyes on Jesus Christ, do it, because there is a confrontation in society, and you need to be ready. The conflict is spiritual in nature, but it manifests itself in the physical realm, and we are not called to fear, but to power and love and a sound mind.[7]

In 2 Chronicles 20:12, Israel had all these enemies coming against her. So King Jehoshaphat prayed and said, "God . . . we do not know what to do, but we are looking to you for help" (*NLT*). Likewise, we declare that we don't have all the answers for the problems in our society today. We don't have all the answers for the pluralism and the increasing dichotomy, nor the syncretism. And we say, "Lord, we don't know what to do, but our eyes are on You."

Win Against Flesh

Hebrews 11:24-26 shows us that by faith not only do we win against fear, but we also win against the flesh:

> By faith Moses, when he had grown up, refused to be called the son of Pharaoh's daughter, choosing rather to endure ill-treatment with the people of God than to enjoy the passing pleasures of sin, considering the reproach of Christ greater riches than the treasures of Egypt; for he was looking to the reward.

---

7. See 2 Timothy 1:7, *KJV*.

Moses *chose* to endure "ill treatment with"—literally in the Greek "to have bad times with"—God's people rather than to enjoy all the pleasures that were laid before him as the son of Pharaoh's daughter. He made a faith decision. And we make faith decisions like that every day in our own lives. Moses chose to value the things of God above the things of the world. He chose to have hard times with the people of God in the service of God rather than to have passing good times in the house of Pharaoh. And when it says the "passing pleasures of sin," it's not just referring to gross sins and sexual immorality; it's talking about power and prestige and possessions and wealth. Those things, in and of themselves, are not wrong. In fact, they're morally neutral. People often say, "Money is the root of all evil." That's not what the Bible says. The Bible says, "The love of money is the root of all sorts of evil."[8] There's a vast difference. Money is nothing. It's the *love* of money that perverts the heart of a man or a woman. Every day we must make a faith decision as to whether we will serve God or mammon, as Jesus said.[9] You can't have two masters. Moses realized that he needed to lay down the passing pleasures of being in the house of Pharaoh to obey God and participate in His purpose for the house of Israel. That was a big deal.

How We Win by Faith

As we choose, in faith, to follow Jesus and become a child of God, we find the power to win against the lure of the world. First John 5:4 says, "For whatever is born of God overcomes the world; and this is the victory that has overcome the world—our faith." It's your faith—faith in the power of Jesus and the preferability of His way—that will help you stand firm. Faith will cause us to hold right values and to make the right decisions. In faith, we can have a proper view of wealth. We can have a proper view of power and prestige and position and possessions

---

8. 1 Timothy 6:10.
9. See Matthew 6:24.

because we esteem the things of God as greater, as being of surpassing value, a "lasting inheritance" as the New Testament puts it.

Moses thought it was better to suffer for the sake of Christ than to own the treasures of Egypt. He made that faith decision because he knew his calling. And there's a call on each of us as well, a call to weigh the promises of the world against the promises of Christ and to make a meaningful decision between them. And that decision will direct the course of your life, so don't make it quickly or flippantly. Don't buy into the hype. Really think about what life in Christ means, and the promises of a life in salvation. Consider it carefully. And then think about the things of the world. Now you might just end up like Abraham, with God making you incredibly wealthy after all. But you might not. Either way, praise the Lord! That's the right view.

Moses left the palace and never went back to his old way of life. He had seen the best the world had to offer. He'd been there, done that. He laid it all down for the purposes of God when he chose to be identified with the Jewish slaves instead of the Egyptian royal family. In our own context, we make similar decisions every single day. With that in mind, 1 John 2:15-17 gives us a scary warning:

Do not love the world nor the things in the world. If anyone loves the world, the love of the Father is not in him. For all that is in the world, the lust of the flesh and the lust of the eyes and the boastful pride of life, is not from the Father, but is from the world. The world is passing away, and also its lusts; but the one who does the will of God lives forever.

That word "love" that's used there is the word *agape*. In this context it means, "Don't seek to find your identity, your joy and your satisfaction in the things of the world." It doesn't mean that you can't say, "Oh, I love my guitars and surfboards," "I love my car." The passage simply means that you are not to seek to find your identity, your purpose, your joy and your satisfaction in those things. In fact—and this is why that passage from 1 John is so scary—it says if you do that, the love of the Father is not in you. There's some sort of disconnect. Now, here's why that worries me personally. It's because I'm so susceptible to doing that. I can easily start trying to find joy and satisfaction in material things, in recognition, in how many friends I have on Facebook. That's just how we are as people.

Passion, Possession and Position

But the Bible tells me, "Don't give in to that." You see, by faith we win over the flesh. Notice what it says in 1 John 2:16: "The lusts of the flesh and the lust of the eyes and the boastful pride of life." All temptation from the enemy falls into those three *Ps*: passion, possession and position. Check it. What are you being tempted with? Where's your flesh yearning? See if it doesn't fall underneath one of these three headings.

It's the same thing that Satan got Eve with in the Garden. In Genesis 3 it says that when she saw the fruit was good for food (passion), a delight to the eyes (possession) and desirable to make one wise (position), she ate of the fruit. Satan doesn't have any new tricks—but the same old tricks still work! Passion, possession and position. The Bible says to be aware of letting your heart get entangled with these things. When you find yourself pursuing them above and beyond and in place of the purposes of God, you are on dangerous ground. Do an about-face, turn around, reconnect with God, and get right.

Regarding my family's surfboard business, the plan was for me to take over the business from my father. Once, during those years when I was trying to juggle the surfboard business and the ministry, I was in England to teach the Bible. I remember talking with God, saying, "Okay, listen, God. You want me to do this whole ministry thing? That's cool. I'll keep teaching and discipling. I'm cool with that. But here's the deal, Lord. See, my parents want to hand the surfboard business over to me. And it's a really good one. It's one of the biggest ones in the world. I don't know if You know this, Lord, but magazines like

TransWorld and *Surfer* call me and ask for interviews. Some of the best surfers in the world are coming to my shaping room to talk to me. There's also some pretty good cash that comes along with the business, Lord—more money than there is in the ministry, that's for dang sure. So here's the deal, Lord. I'll do the ministry thing, but You need what I've got. Think about the possessions, the position, and the influence I could have for You, Lord, if I was a world famous surfboard maker like my dad is. That way I could really impact the world for You. I could do so much more ministry. Lord, You *need* this surfboard business!"

I told these things to the Lord. He replied through the life of Moses, "Britt, Moses had a really good surfboard business. It was called the house of Pharaoh. He had more position, more power, more prestige than you've ever imagined. But for Me to use him, I had to take him out of the house of Pharaoh and make him a shepherd before he could do anything for My glory. Put it on the altar, Britt."

In the flesh, that was a very hard thing to do. The surfboard business meant fame and prestige and money and fun. It was hard to put that on the altar. But by faith we win over the flesh.

Remember, faith is believing in the value of certain things over the value of other things and then making decisions accordingly. So by grace and the mercy of God I decided the kingdom of God and the work of God were more important for me than surfboards.

Win Against the Foe

Hebrews 11:28-29 shows us that by faith we can win against our foe:

> By faith he kept the Passover and the sprinkling of the blood, so that he who destroyed the firstborn would not touch them. By faith they passed through the Red Sea as though they were passing through dry land; and the Egyptians, when they attempted it, were drowned.

First, we need to know that we *do* have a foe. His name is Satan, and he wants to mess up our lives. If he cannot get us to hell because we are Christians, then he wants to make our lives hell here and now. He wants to get us caught up in sexual immorality; he wants us in bad relationships; he wants us pursuing passions and possessions and position. He wants to complicate the simplicity of our lives in Christ. He wants to rip us off of the joy and the peace and the satisfaction that are found in obeying Jesus Christ. And he's real serious about it. First Peter 5:8-9 says:

> Be of sober spirit, be on the alert. Your adversary, the devil, prowls around like a roaring lion, seeking someone to devour. But resist him, firm in your faith, knowing that the same experiences of suffering are being accomplished by your brethren who are in the world.

You have to make faith decisions because the enemy is looking to rip you off. Jesus said in John 10:10, "[Satan] comes only to steal and kill and destroy; I came that they might have life, and have it abundantly." So there are daily decisions that are made according to that promise. First John 3:8 says that "the Son of God appeared for this purpose, to destroy the works of the devil." Are you letting Jesus systematically do that in your life? Are you letting Him overcome and destroy the work of the enemy that tries to come against every Christian? He's already accomplished it on the cross, as Colossians 2:13-15 tells us.

> When you were dead in your transgressions and the uncircumcision of your flesh, He made you alive together with Him, having forgiven us all our transgressions, having canceled out the certificate of debt consisting of decrees against us, which was hostile to us; and He has taken it out of the way, having nailed it to the cross. When He had disarmed the rulers and authorities, He made a public display of them, having triumphed over them through Him.

So the Bible says that Satan (the chief of those "rulers and authorities" in verse 15) is a defeated foe. Jesus Christ defeated him on the cross and through the resurrection. "Defeated" is past tense, but it has a present result. It is a done deal *and* it has an immediate, tangible effect on your life today when you live by faith.

In Ephesians 6:11-17, Paul tells us how to fend off the enemy, beginning in verse 11: "Put on the full armor of God, so that you will be able to stand firm against the schemes of the devil." Specifically, when attacks come, the piece of armor that verse 16 tells us to take up is "the shield of faith with which you will be able to extinguish all the flaming arrows of the evil one." Faith is our shield against the foe and renders his attacks powerless. Faith takes the fire out of his flaming arrows and sends them falling to the ground. We stand behind the shield of faith, safe and secure in Christ.

Satan Wants You Back

Remember the old Army posters with Uncle Sam pointing his finger at you with the slogan underneath "I Want You For The U.S. Army"? Satan uses that same slogan for his band of misfits. When you decide to make an exodus out of that lifestyle of slavery, Satan *will* come and try to get you back. Colossians 1:13-14 says:

> For He rescued us from the domain of darkness, and transferred us to the kingdom of His beloved Son, in whom we have redemption, the forgiveness of sins.

When God rescues us, we transfer to a new location. An exodus happens, much like that of Moses and the children of Israel, to the winning side. But the enemy doesn't always give up that easily. That's why it says in Ephesians 4:27, "Do not give the devil an opportunity." In the Greek, that word "opportunity" is *topos*—the same root from which we get our word "topography." The word generally means *place* or *space*. Here it carries the idea of *a favorable circumstance for doing something.*

Don't give Satan a favorable circumstance in your life, because he'll jump all over it. He is opportunistic and he is a squatter. He has no legal right in the life of the Christian, but if we give him ground, then he will tie down, hold down, hunker down, set up camp, and create a stronghold. Don't give the enemy an inch! Know that he prowls around like a roaring lion, looking for someone to devour. And if you are endeavoring to continue in the exodus and walk out of slavery and into the promises of God, Satan will come after you with the full power of hell. But by faith we win over the foe. By faith we know that Satan is a defeated enemy.

Fear and Forgetfulness

When attack came upon the Israelites, check out their response in Exodus 14:11-12:

> Then they said to Moses, "Is it because there were no graves in Egypt that you have taken us away to die in the wilderness? Why have you dealt with us in this way, bringing us out of Egypt? Is this not the word that we spoke to you in Egypt, saying, 'Leave us alone that we may serve the Egyptians'? For it would have been better for us to serve the Egyptians than to die in the wilderness."

Wow, is that ridiculous or what? And that is so you and me when the enemy is messing with us. We immediately begin to say, "It doesn't pay to serve God. It's so hard to do the right thing. Life was so easy before and now it's hard." We do the same thing the Israelites did. They said, "Why did you bring us out of Egypt? What are you doing, trying to kill us?" Did they forget that Pharaoh was slaughtering their children and burdening them and killing them and that they were slaves? Yeah, they forgot. I forget what the slavery of the old life was like. And on occasion I flirt with it and I need a reminder. *Don't go there! Don't go*

188

back to Egypt. In our fear, we lose perspective. But we don't need to be afraid of the enemy. He's a defeated foe! Be strong in the strength of the Lord and in His might. All that the enemy has on you, Christian, is intimidation! If you haven't given him a foothold, then all he has on you is intimidation. But if we forget that, and give in to that fear, we lose perspective and we start thinking, *Yeah, I was better off in Egypt.*

Moses' Pep Talk

Moses responds to the Israelites in Exodus 14:13-14 with a good pep talk:

> But Moses said to the people, "Do not fear! Stand by and see the salvation of the LORD which He will accomplish for you today; for the Egyptians whom you have seen today, you will never see them again forever. The LORD will fight for you while you keep silent."

"Stand by" in verse 13 could also be translated, "Take your stand!" Basically, Moses said, "Get up, you wussies! Take your stand and watch the Lord do what the Lord does!" The Israelites needed to hear that pep talk at that moment. They needed that proclamation of faith and trust in the Lord. Watch what happens next in verses 21-25:

> Then Moses stretched out his hand over the sea; and the LORD swept the sea back by a strong east wind all night and turned the sea into dry land, so the waters were divided. The sons of Israel went through the midst of the sea on the dry land, and the waters were like a wall to them on their right hand and on their left. Then the Egyptians took up the pursuit [here comes the enemy] and all Pharaoh's horses, his chariots and his horsemen went in after them into the midst of the sea. At the morning watch, the LORD looked down on the army of the Egyptians through the pillar of fire and cloud and brought the army of the Egyptians into confusion. He caused their chariot wheels

to swerve, and He made them drive with difficulty; so the Egyptians said, "Let us flee from Israel, for the LORD is fighting for them against the Egyptians."

The enemy said, "We've got to get out of here!" What does James 4:7 say? "Resist the devil and he will flee from you." Take your stand, trust in the Lord, be strong in the strength of the Lord. Your enemy will flee from you, because the Lord fights on your behalf! And flee is exactly what Pharaoh and his army did. We see it in Exodus 14:26-29:

> Then the LORD said to Moses, "Stretch out your hand over the sea so that the waters may come back over the Egyptians, over their chariots and their horsemen." So Moses stretched out his hand over the sea, and the sea returned to its normal state at daybreak, while the Egyptians were fleeing right into it; then the LORD overthrew the Egyptians in the midst of the sea. The waters returned and covered the chariots and the horsemen, even Pharaoh's entire army that had gone into the sea after them; not even one of them remained. But the sons of Israel walked on dry land.

It has said "dry land" now about three times. When God does it, it's not mucky; it's not muddy; it's not slimy. It's dry; it's solid. On Christ, the solid rock, we stand. As we see in verses 29-31, the Israelites walked through on dry land:

> Through the midst of the sea, and the waters were like a wall to them on their right hand and on their left. Thus the LORD saved Israel that day from the hand of the Egyptians, and Israel saw the Egyptians dead on the seashore. When Israel saw the great power which the LORD had used against the Egyptians, the people feared the LORD, and they believed in the LORD and in His servant Moses.

When the Israelites saw the victory of God, they chose to fear God alone, and to believe in Him. Have we today not seen the victory of Christ on the cross? How can we fear anyone other than Jesus Christ? We fear Jesus Christ and serve Him alone, and we believe Him. And what we believe about Him affects the daily decisions that we make. We believe that He is victorious. In fact, Moses wrote a song about that. You can see Moses' song in Exodus 15:1-3:

> Then Moses and the sons of Israel sang this song to the LORD, and said, "I will sing to the LORD, for He is highly exalted; the horse and its rider He has hurled into the sea. The LORD is my strength and song, and He has become my salvation; this is my God, and I will praise Him; my father's God, and I will extol Him. The LORD is a warrior; the LORD is His name."

The Lord is a warrior! He fights on behalf of His people. What are you afraid of—and what do you believe God can do about it? What do you desire? And do you believe that Jesus Christ is better than it? What lies is the enemy telling you? And is not the truth of God stronger and better? Does it not dispel the lie? By faith we win because Christ has won. That is our song.

10

FAITH WELCOMING

Rahab

By faith the walls of Jericho fell down after they had been encircled for seven days. By faith Rahab the harlot did not perish along with those who were disobedient, after she had welcomed the spies in peace.

HEBREWS 11:30-31

I CAN RELATE TO RAHAB. Her story was particularly relevant to me when I had to choose between staying in our family business or going into the ministry. I've mentioned my experience with that time of waiting and wondering like Sarah and Abraham had. My wife, Kate, and I had to put it on the altar like Abraham put Isaac so that we could surrender and give it up to God.

Then there came a time for Kate and me of welcoming God's purposes in our lives, like Rahab. The Lord brought us to this place before everything was clear, where we said, "Okay, Lord, we'll go anywhere and do anything You want us to do. We've been holding on to this surfboard thing so tightly, but we believe that You're right and that Your purpose and Your mission are bigger and that You're good. And so, Lord, we'll go anywhere You want us to go, and we'll do whatever You want us to do."

There came a real moment when Kate and I prayed that together one night. Never in my wildest imagination would I have thought that God would let me stay in my hometown, which I love more than any place in the whole world, and I've been around the world a few times! Never would I have dreamed that God would let me stay here in Carpinteria and serve Him, that He'd let me preach the gospel here, that Kate and I would get to raise our kids here, that we'd get to be in the ministry here. All of this is beyond anything I ever would have thought to ask. And He gave me all of it, and more.

But what He did for Rahab was infinitely greater. He blessed her for believing He was true and right and good in His purposes. In Rahab we see faith that welcomes the purposes of God. Hebrews 11:31 says that *by faith* Rahab welcomed the spies that Joshua sent to check out Jericho, the land that God had promised to Israel. Rahab recognized God was doing something wonderful and extraordinary in her lifetime and in her locale.

Rahab believed God was true and right and good in His purposes. That's why she welcomed God's purposes in her life by faith. Let's not pull any punches here. *Very few Christians actually welcome the purposes of*

God, the mission of God, in their lives. We see the evidence of this in many ways. First, take a look around the local church and see who's serving. In almost any local church, you'll find that about 10 percent of the people do 90 percent of the work. That's certainly true in the church where I pastor. The majority of people in any church are pew potatoes. Occasionally these potatoes may sprout a little something, but mostly they just sit there. If you're part of a church community, but never became a *contributing* part of that community, you're like a baby or a suckerfish. You're feeding on the milk, you're sucking, you're taking, but you haven't crossed the threshold of giving. That's the unfortunate reality in most churches.

Second, shifting from a micro to a macro perspective, you can see that very few Christians welcome the purposes and the mission of God in their lives by how many Christians are involved in ministry on a world scale. There are about 2.2 billion Christians in the world, but only about 12 million are involved in ministry, and that includes both clergy *and* lay people.[1] If you do the math, it means that worldwide only about .55 percent of Christians are doing any sort of ministry. A little more than one half of 1 percent! And that means that more than 99 percent of Christians—99.45 percent to be exact—are *not* engaged in ministry or mission.

You Are Gifted and Called

The Bible clearly teaches that every member is a minister. It's called the doctrine of the priesthood of the saints from 1 Peter 2. Every Christian is called, every Christian is anointed, and every Christian is gifted.[2] Every Christian is called to be on mission for the purposes of God—to see that men and women, boys and girls around the world hear the good news that God loves them. We are each called to share the news

---

1. David B. Barret and Todd M. Johnson, International Bulletin of Missionary Research, January 2009. http://www.gordonconwell.edu/ockenga/globalchristianity/resources.php.

2. See 1 Peter 4:10.

that Jesus Christ is the only, unique Savior of the world and that through His death on the cross and His resurrection from the dead, we are saved from sin and its penalties, sin and its bondage, sin and its agents, and sin and its consequences—namely, death. We are called to proclaim that Jesus Christ saves and transforms and renews in the here and now and delivers us to heaven when we leave this earth. And in addition to, but before, going to heaven when we die, we are invited to enjoy and manifest, proclaim and participate in the kingdom of heaven in *this* lifetime. Every Christian is gifted and called to this mission in some capacity, but the vast majority of Christians are not in any way engaged in it going forth. So many are missing the mission of God in their lives.

God Is Up to Something Big

In Rahab's time and during the few decades that encompass the book of Joshua, God was up to something extraordinary. We'll look at that in a moment. But first, we need to recognize that God has also been up to something extraordinary in *our* times—in just the last few decades. Do you realize that more people have followed Christ in the last 100 years than in all the previous centuries combined?[3] Yet more than 6,000 unreached people groups live in the world today.[4] That is good news, and there is good reason to be optimistic in regards to the Great Commission and the mission of God today. Even though there's still a lot of work to be done, it is good to recognize that God is up to something big. Despite what you might hear in the media, evangelical Christianity is currently the fastest growing religious movement worldwide. The growth rate of evangelical Christianity *doubles* that of Islam in the

3. Steven C. Hawthorne, *Perspectives on the World Christian Movement: The Study Guide* (Pasadena, CA: William Carey Library, 2009), p. 73.
4. See "Global Summary, The Joshua Project," http://www.joshuaproject.net/; and "Unreached People Groups," Global Frontier Missions, http://www.globalfrontiermissions.com/people groups/unreached.html.

world. More good news: The growth rate of evangelical Christianity is *triple* that of the population growth![5]

And yet about 27 percent of the world's 6 billion people or more are still unreached with the message.[6] In the last 15 years, about 1 million churches have been planted. That's great news! But we need millions more. God is on the move and accomplishing His purposes in this world. And this world involves *your* world. Questions that every sincere, authentic Christian must ask include: *Am I welcoming God's purposes? Am I welcoming God's mission? Am I involved by faith in what God is doing? Do I really have faith that believes certain things about the character of God, the person of Christ and the mission of God—a faith that causes me to rethink my life?*

That's what it means to have faith that results in life change, a trust that transforms. As Christians, we believe certain things about the person and the character and the work of God that cause us to rethink our priorities, finances, sexuality, relationships, grudges, and recreation. All of these things are to be rethought in light of the mission of God and His calling on your life.

Rahab understood that principle. She welcomed God's purposes and got involved. But before we go there, let's revisit the backstory. First of all, there's the slavery of Israel and their exodus out of Egypt. Israel's backs were being beaten and their children murdered, so they cried out to God. God heard their cry and raised up Moses as their leader. With an outstretched arm and a strong right hand, God Himself delivered Israel out of Egypt, got them across the Red Sea, led them through the wilderness, and brought them to a place on the southern portion of Canaan, the Promised Land, called Kadesh Barnea. It was there that Israel was to enter into the promises and rest of God. But remember, they failed to do so because of their lack of faith, their lack of belief. They

---

5. Jason Mandryk, "The State of the Gospel" in *Perspectives on the World Christian Movement Reader* (Pasadena, CA: William Carey Library, 2009), p. 362.

6. Ibid., p. 367.

simply didn't trust! They saw the circumstances, they saw the giants, they saw the walled cities, and in response they allowed the drama and the difficulties to be bigger in their minds than their God.[7]

Is Your God Bigger than Your Drama?

God is *always* bigger than our drama, my brothers and sisters. But we can lose perspective from time to time, can't we? Things begin to seem so big and intimidating that we lose trust in our big God. Israel lost it and they said, "No, we don't think God's going to pull it off."

Because of that unbelief, they were judged. God always blesses belief. God also judges unbelief. God had demonstrated His goodness and His faithfulness to Israel so many times, yet they still didn't trust. But that unbelieving generation died out, and Moses died. Then a new leader, Joshua, rose to the forefront of Israel. Joshua comes on the scene at a time when the children of Israel are brought into the blessings and the promises and the fruitful place of God—the land of Canaan that He reserved for them. Five hundred years of prophetic history push at the back of Israel and their new, young leader Joshua. There they are, camped out at the Jordan River for three days, just to see how wide it was, how swiftly it flowed and how difficult it would be to get a million and a half people across. They knew it would be impossible unless God did something extraordinary. They believed that He would.

And He did. He stopped up the river a mile upstream. Scripture tells us that the river stood up in a heap and they walked through on dry land.[8] The people of Israel experienced the promises of God by the power of God—a powerful picture of the Christian life. By faith they entered into the good place where God wanted them. But they still had obstacles to overcome by faith—namely, the walls of Jericho. God gave them specific instructions to get past those big walls. Not only

---

7. See Numbers 13–14.
8. See Joshua 3:13-17.

were those instructions specific, but they were also just plain weird. God can be weird. His ways are not our ways. He told Joshua and the people of Israel to march around the city seven times, all those days in a row and not to say anything at all. Then at an appointed time, they were to shout and blow the trumpet, causing the walls to come falling down. It happened just as God said it would.

Here's what I want you to grasp from that whole story: God was clearly on the move during that time. He was on the move for His purposes, for His glory and for the benefit of His people. God's purposes and mission were going forward. And what is God's mission? It is for Him to bless all the nations and to be glorified in every nation. Genesis 12:2-3 helps explain that mission when it says that God blessed Abraham so that he would be a blessing to others, and through Abraham, God would bless all the "families of the earth." Blessing the nations is part of the purpose and the mission of God. It is also God's plan that He be glorified. That's why when we see a snapshot of heaven in Revelation 7, it is every tongue, tribe and nation worshiping the Lamb of God who sits on the throne.

But here in the book of Joshua, God accomplishes His purpose of blessing all the nations by first revealing Himself to and then through one particular nation—the nation of Israel. We see God assert Himself over and against the pagan beliefs, gods and practices of the land of Canaan that held people in bondage. God, because He's a deliverer, because He's a lover, because He wants to set people free from the bondage of the enemy and the bondage of the flesh, asserts His power over these false gods. We see it in the book of Joshua, and we still see it today. God is constantly asserting Himself in fresh, new ways, doing good works for His own glory, and showing His power to break strongholds and set people free.

At Reality, the church of which I am pastor, we have been seeing that happen in many profound ways lately. Recently, a fortuneteller was to open a shop just a few blocks away from the church. We saw a "Coming Soon" sign in the little storefront. So we brought it before the people of the church and asked them to pray, saying, "This is not going to happen in our community. We don't want deception and darkness that bring bondage. We want the truth to go forth. We want the light that brings freedom."

A few weeks later I drove down Linden Avenue in Carpinteria and that fortuneteller's name had disappeared. The "Coming Soon" sign had been replaced by a "Space Available" sign. Nothing against that lady fortuneteller—I don't hate her. I pray for her salvation. But it's the spiritual reality behind those things. This is serious business, because people's lives are at stake.

God Works Through People

Likewise, God didn't hate the Canaanites; He hated the demonic false gods that kept them in bondage. So He asserted Himself over and against them. He kept moving His purpose forward. But here's the thing about God's purpose and God's mission: Throughout history, God—in His great wisdom—has chosen to work *through* people rather than *independent* of people. In some cases it even appears that God will, or will not, do certain things *depending on human participation*. For example, in Ezekiel 22, Israel was in trouble with God again. They were disobeying, and as a result, they were about to be rightly judged and chastened by God. Instead, before God carried out His judgment, He first looked for someone who would intercede. In Ezekiel 22:30, God says:

> I searched for a man among them who would build up the wall and stand in the gap before Me for the land, so that I would not destroy it; but I found no one.

God looked for an intercessor like Moses in Exodus 32. Remember the story? When Moses was on Mount Sinai, Israel began to fornicate around this false god, a golden calf, that they had made for themselves. God said, "Hey, Moses, get down the mountain, man. Your people are going nuts-o. Move it, because I'm about to wipe them out." God would have been totally justified in His judgment against them. But Moses reasoned with God, telling Him why He shouldn't destroy the people. He interceded, "Lord, I ask that You would have mercy on them, not because they deserve it, but for Your great name. Have mercy on them!" So God relented. He turned from that undesired course of judgment and had mercy on an entire generation and a nation *because one man asked.*

The Search for Someone with Faith

In Ezekiel 22:31, God looked for someone to do the same. But there was nobody to intercede for the people of Jerusalem, nobody to plead for mercy. So God judged the people instead:

> "Thus I have poured out My indignation on them; I have consumed them with the fire of My wrath; their way I have brought upon their heads," declares the LORD God.

God's willingness to work through people rather than independent of people does not negate His sovereignty. Rather it is an expression of that sovereignty. It says that in His power, God has chosen to involve humanity. Because He has done so, humanity is now responsible. These two ideas that we see repeatedly in Scripture (that God is sovereign and man is responsible) are compatible in this way: God's sovereignty never functions to mitigate man's responsibility, and man's responsibility never functions to diminish God's sovereignty.[9] So, as an act of His sovereignty, God makes people responsible to pray and participate in His work.

And so because of God's choice to involve people, here's what we see throughout history: We see God *looking* for men and women who are

---

9. For this idea, I am indebted to D. A. Carson, *Divine Sovereignty and Human Responsibility: Biblical Perspectives in Tension* (Eugene, OR: Wipf and Stock Publishers, 2002).

willing to be used for His purposes. God went looking and found Noah, Abraham, Moses, Peter and Paul. When God looks, will He find you?

God Found Rahab

God looked and found Rahab in that state of faith. What made Rahab suitable and ready for God's purposes? And what makes us suitable and ready for God's purposes as well? We find the answer in Joshua 2—the story of Jericho. The story begins in verse 1:

> Then Joshua the son of Nun sent two men as spies secretly from Shittim, saying, "Go, view the land, especially Jericho." So they went and came into the house of a harlot whose name was Rahab, and lodged there.

The first thing we see here—and it is repeated in Hebrews 11—is that Rahab was a prostitute. So then, was it her moral character that made her ready and suitable for God's purposes? No. It wasn't an issue of her moral character, though Scripture teaches us that God *is* concerned about moral character. But that wasn't what qualified Rahab. In the next seven verses we discover Rahab is a liar as well. So what qualified her for the work God planned? Joshua 2:8-11 reveals the answer:

> Now before they lay down, she came up to them on the roof, and said to the men, "I know that the LORD has given you the land, and that the terror of you has fallen on us, and that all the inhabitants of the land have melted away before you. For we have heard how the LORD dried up the water of the Red Sea before you when you came out of Egypt, and what you did to the two kings of the Amorites who were beyond the Jordan, to Sihon and Og, whom you utterly destroyed. When we heard it, our hearts melted and no courage remained in any man any longer because of you; for the LORD your God, He is God in heaven above and on earth beneath."

Rahab believed God. She had faith, even as a lying prostitute. She didn't quite have her morals all together yet. She wasn't well trained in the right approach to ministry. She still had things to learn. But remember, she didn't know the Word of God. She hadn't been instructed in the truth of God that came from Mount Sinai. And you have to consider the culture that she came from. Canaanite culture was famous for, among other things, placing live babies in jars and then building them into the foundations of buildings as "foundation sacrifices."[10]

This is the culture from which she came. So it probably wasn't very unusual to be a prostitute, and lying to save the spies was probably not a real big deal for her in regard to her conscience. I'm not saying that sin is right, but we might want to cut her some slack. After all, God did. And she had faith. In verse 9 she says, "I know that the LORD has given you the land," and in verse 11 she says, "the LORD your God, He is God in heaven above and on earth beneath."

Why God Chose Rahab

Rahab was chosen because she recognized the God of Israel over and against all the false gods and the pagan gods of the Canaanite culture. She said, "This is the one true God." She had faith, and it came from what she had heard. In verse 10 she says, "For we have heard," and again, in verse 11, "When we heard."

What does Romans 10:17 say to you and me? "So faith comes from hearing and hearing by the Word of Christ." The Word of God increases faith. When we read it, when we consume it, when we study it, when we listen to it, faith is increased. Faith is developed the same way in our lives as it was in the life of Rahab. She heard these things about God—these incredible stories of His great power—and she

---

10. John MacArthur, Jr., *The MacArthur New Testament Commentary (Hebrews)* (Chicago, IL: Moody Press, 1983), p. 364.

believed them. That yielded in her a faith that recognized who God was and caused her to be submitted to His purposes.

Do you realize how profound this was? The whole city had heard the stories. Notice that Rahab said, "*We* have heard what God did and who He is," and yet it appears from the account that she was the only one in the city that believed. They had all heard the same thing, but not all believed. No one else had the faith that Rahab did. And that's true today—of Christians and non-Christians alike. Two Christians could hear the same message, read the same passage, and one could respond in faith and experience a transformed life and the other one just walk away indifferent and unchanged. Two non-Christians could hear the exact same message—the gospel message—and one of them could say, "I believe it" and experience a radically transformed life, while the other person just shrugs their shoulders and says, "Good for you."

That perplexes some people, me included, at times. All I know is what the Bible says: that God is revealed, that God pursues, that God woos, that God draws by His Holy Spirit, and that we need to receive that. Some people do, and some people don't. That's what happened in Rahab's culture. Everyone heard the same message, but only Rahab believed.

Will You Believe?

What is often surprising to me—though I don't understand it—is who chooses to believe. Jesus, in the Gospel accounts, dealt with the religious leaders, the chief priests and the elders of the Jewish faith. These people should have been in the know, should have had the greatest faith. Yet it was to them that He said in Matthew 21:31-32:

> Truly I say to you that the tax collectors[11] and prostitutes will
> get into the kingdom of God before you. For John [the Baptist]

---

11. Remember that in the time this was written, tax collectors were the worst kind of traitor. They were considered extortionists and were the outcasts of society, not like the IRS today. (Kind of.)

came to you in the way of righteousness and you did not believe him; but the tax collectors and prostitutes did believe him.

The tax collectors and prostitutes believed the message. Yet the message was lost on the religious people for one reason or another. We could write several books just on why. But the people who *knew* they were in need—the people who understood their brokenness or understood their failure, the marginalized, the disenfranchised, the tax collectors, the prostitutes, and me and some of you—we have all said, "Wait a minute, I have a need. I'm not perfect, but there is a perfect God who made me. I'm accountable to Him. I need to repent of the things I've done wrong and receive the forgiveness of Jesus Christ through His cross." Jesus pointed to the religious people and said, "You guys are not getting into the kingdom of God before these prostitutes and these tax collectors." Another time, He said, "It's not the healthy who need a physician; it's the sick. I didn't come to call the righteous, but sinners."[12] He came to seek and to save that which was lost.[13]

Perhaps Rahab was just lost enough in that society, just marginalized enough, that when she heard about the God who delivered Israel from slavery in Egypt, it meant something to her. It resonated with her when she heard about a God who was kind, merciful, powerful and not like the dumb idols her people would pray to all day long yet never see *do* anything. This God sounded nothing like the false gods that kept her people in bondage. Maybe she was just broken enough that when she heard the story of this other God who was alive and moving and powerful, she knew she needed Him.

Who knows what happened in Rahab's life to land her in the life of a prostitute. Everybody's got a story. While I don't think that prostitution was too unusual in Canaanite society, I'm pretty sure it still wasn't respectable or honored. Maybe she was abandoned by her dad,

12. Mark 2:17; Luke 5:32.
13. See Luke 19:10.

or forgotten by her mom. Who knows what degree of brokenness was in her life? Does it matter? We're broken people. And so when we hear the story, this truth about a God who cares, a God who saves and delivers and restores, a God who would stop the forward momentum of 500 years of prophetic history to call a prostitute into a brand-new life and community, that means something to us, because we see ourselves in Rahab.

Why Do We Miss It?

And so we have to ask ourselves why we don't welcome the purposes of God. It seems like more than 99 percent of Christians don't. Why? Well, first of all, probably because it's inconvenient, but that's the norm. It's almost always inconvenient to welcome the purposes of God. Just look at Rahab's story. Welcoming God's purposes rocked her world—literally! The walls that she lived in were going to shake all around her and the world that she knew would crumble and burn. That certainly wasn't convenient. But it was the purpose of God that would radically change the world.

Things would never be the same again when the walls of Jericho came down. This is often what happens when God calls people. He called Peter, James and John and said, "Hey, guys, come and follow Me,"[14] and they dropped their nets and followed Him. These weren't nets that belonged to someone else. They were in a family fishing business—those were *their* nets. They had to drop those things that they owned—those things with which they earned their living—leave them behind and follow Jesus. Then there was Matthew, sitting at his little collection booth collecting taxes, and Jesus said, "Hey, Matthew! You, come on, follow Me."[15] Matthew had to leave that life behind—not only all the practical aspects of it, but the identity that came along

---

14. See Luke 5:1-11.
15. See Matthew 9:9.

with it as well. Although inconvenient, leaving was the best thing he ever did.

We Americans don't like inconvenience. Don't inconvenience me. Don't trouble me. Don't bug me. That's us Americans. Like you, I want everything to go smoothly and orderly and easily. Let's be honest—that's just who we are. There is no one that says, "Awesome! I'm so inconvenienced right now. This is great. Oh, bless the Lord. I'm just all jacked up right now. This is wonderful." No one likes to be inconvenienced.

Our Comfort Comes First

A recent study by The Barna Group states that 70 percent of Americans say that having a comfortable lifestyle is very important to them.[16] I'd say about 30 percent of Americans lied! Apparently more Americans are becoming honest because the number rose from 59 percent in 1991.[17] That's a dramatic increase in just a few years of people who would say that having a comfortable lifestyle is very important. On the other hand, only 56 percent of Americans say that making a difference in the world is important to them.[18] The reality is that nearly half the people out there don't give a rip whether or not they make a difference in this world. More astoundingly, only 45 percent of Americans say that being active in church is very important to them.[19]

So what we have is a conflict in values. What we value most for ourselves is not necessarily that which God values most for us. Now understand, I'm just like you. I want to be comfortable, and I hate to be inconvenienced just as much as you do. But we have a real problem here, because our values as Americans are not aligned with the

---

16. "Survey Details Current Vision of the American Dream," The Barna Group, June 23, 2008. https://www.barna.org/barna-update/article/14-media/33-survey-details-current-vision-of-the-american-dream.

17. Ibid.

18. Ibid.

19. Ibid.

values of God. And don't tell me that you think the numbers would be different if the survey was done only within the Church. The statistical difference in the behaviors of Christians and non-Christians in America is almost indistinguishable on every account—unless those Christians read their Bibles and allow their understanding of the Bible to shape their worldview.[20]

The numbers are eerily similar for addiction to pornography, adultery and all sorts of sin. The majority of the Church is almost indistinguishable from the rest of society. So the Church has a real cultural conflict. We highly value comfort—something that God does not necessarily highly value for us. His mission is more important than our comfort or convenience. So as a whole, we just aren't ready to welcome the purposes of God because our desire for comfort and convenience is greater than our desire for God's mission.

Following God Is Not a Risk-Free Offer

The second reason we often don't welcome the purposes of God is because of the risk associated with it. If the king had found out that Rahab had lied to him, he would have killed her. So for Rahab, there was significant risk associated with welcoming the purposes of God. Same with Moses. Moses had to go and stand before Pharaoh and say, "Um, Pharaoh, God said you need to let My people go." There was some real risk associated with that. Very few of us are willing to risk *anything* for God in Christian culture today, much less put our lives on the line. We value our "security," which is only an illusion anyway, as we discussed in chapter 5. We think of our perceived security as being more important than God's purposes—because nobody wants to risk for God these days.

Another reason we don't walk in the purposes of God is sin—particularly selfishness. Rahab's actions were not selfish. If she was concerned about herself, she would have exposed the spies and not risked

---

20. George Barna, *Think Like Jesus* (Nashville, TN: Thomas Nelson, 2005).

getting herself in trouble with the king. When she welcomed the purposes of God, we see that she displayed a selfless attitude. She was concerned about God's purposes and her family's wellbeing, if you read the rest of the story.

The next thing that often hinders us is misunderstanding, mainly because most of us are not fully convinced of God's goodness or wisdom. Many of us think that welcoming God's purposes and mission in our life will make us miserable. We must believe that, or the statistics would be different, and the majority of us would welcome His purposes and His mission. The reality is that most of us believe that if we really obey God, it's going to make us miserable. That's entirely untrue. It might make you poor. It might put you in danger. It might even cost you your life—like the 175,000 Christians around the world who will be killed for their faith this year.

Whatever it costs you to follow the purposes of God, I can tell you this: You will not be miserable. Was Stephen miserable when they were stoning him and he opened up his eyes and saw Jesus standing there at the right hand of God to welcome him into glory?[21] I don't think so. Were Paul and Silas miserable when imprisoned for their faith in Philippi? Or when they were worshiping Jesus in the jail cell and even the jailer was converted?[22] I don't think so. I don't think we really trust God and believe that He could satisfy us in adversity. So we inoculate ourselves against adversity—and as a consequence against the fullness of God's plan for us—because of outright misunderstanding.

Another reason we don't welcome the purposes of God is money. That is to say, we are seldom satisfied with how much we have and we usually are not sure how best to use it. There's confusion regarding our finances in the kingdom of God. In John 6, Jesus wanted to feed the 5,000. Testing Philip, He said, "Philip, come here. Philip, you know, we should feed these people." What did Philip revert to? Immediately

---

21. See Acts 7:54-60.
22. See Acts 16:22-30.

he became fearful of the finances involved. Immediately Philip says, "Well, uh, here's the deal, Jesus. I don't think it's gonna work out financially." He tells Jesus that 200 denarii wasn't going to be enough money to feed all the people present.[23] That was his response to the Lord. A denarii was a day's wage, so he was saying that the better part of a year's income is not enough to feed this crowd. What he was really saying was, "I don't think it's going to work this time, Lord."

One more reason that we often miss the purposes of God is our devotion to our own agendas. Put very simply, we just want to do what we want to do—and we don't really want God to interfere with that. We've got plans, hopes, dreams, and stuff that we want to accomplish. The church in Laodicea was like that. Revelation 3:20 says that Jesus stood at the door and knocked and said, "If anyone hears My voice and opens the door, I will come in to him and will dine with him." Yet we have our own agendas; we want to do what we want to do. We say, "Lord, I'll let You in a little bit, but don't go in this room. Don't mess with that area. Don't touch that stuff. Listen, You can have all of this, Lord, just don't touch this. Not right here." That's how we find ourselves in the unenviable position of Jesus knocking on the doors of our hearts, saying, "Hey, if you'll let Me in, I'll really come in and transform your life." We miss that transformative work in our lives—we miss participating in the purpose and the mission of God—because we just want to do what we want to do.

You Can Make a Difference

Statistics say that 75 percent of evangelicals want to make a difference in the world. And yet, as we read earlier, only 0.55 percent (slightly more than one half of 1 percent) actually do something. My guess is that you're different—you really *are* going to make a difference in this world—or you wouldn't be reading this book. You want to see the mission of God go forth. You want to see the Great Commission accom-

---

23. See John 6:5-8.

plished in this generation. You want to see the return of the Lord. But the good news of the gospel must be preached to all the nations first.[24] That starts with faith—with faith that is willing to open up and to welcome the purposes of God no matter what the cost. And with a simple faith like that, this thing becomes so doable.

Think about this scenario: If every Christian in the world led just one person to the Lord, and then discipled them for a year, because we're called to make disciples and not just converts, we'd be on the way. If at the end of that year, each of them led another person to the Lord—just one—and then they discipled that person for a year and then those people in turn each led one person to the Lord, and if the process continued, more than 33 million people would become Christians within 25 years, and within 34 years, the whole world would be evangelized.[25]

Just one a year! That's not great faith; it's just a little bit of faith. It's just faith that says, "Okay, there's this guy and he sits next to me in the truck all day long and we drive around and we do our job. Lord, I'm scared, I'm nervous and there's some relational risk associated with this and some risk to my reputation, but I know that I need to tell him about Your love." Or it may mean saying, "There's this kid at school and they're so messed up and they're so miserable and they're so going down the wrong road and, Jesus, You found me and You changed me. Help me to communicate Your love to them." We can start with just one. What God is up to in our lifetime is way bigger than our fears and our little concerns.

Rahab's life was full of liabilities. She was a prostitute, a woman in a society that did not have great esteem for women, and a Canaanite. And although she had all these things working against her, when it came to the purposes of God, her life was radically transformed. Rahab

---

24. See Matthew 24:14.
25. Michael Bronson, "Addition vs. Multiplication," BibleHelp.org, 1997, 1999 and 2000. http://www.biblehelp.org/addition.htm.

emerges as one of only two women, along with Sarah, in the Hall of Faith. Rahab is also one of only two people that James used to exemplify faith in James 2:25-26. When he wanted to talk about authentic faith, he pointed to two people: Abraham and Rahab. He says about Rahab:

> In the same way, was not Rahab the harlot also justified by works when she received the messengers and sent them out by another way? For just as the body without the spirit is dead, so also faith without works is dead.

James is not talking about becoming righteous by works; he's talking about displaying righteousness by works and showing that we have been made righteous. This third fact is a mind-blower: Rahab is one of only two non-Jews in the genealogy of Christ. Matthew 1:1-6 says this:

> The record of the genealogy of Jesus the Messiah, the son of David, the son of Abraham: Abraham was the father of Isaac, Isaac the father of Jacob, and Jacob the father of Judah and his brothers. Judah was the father of Perez and Zerah by Tamar, Perez was the father of Hezron, and Hezron the father of Ram. Ram was the father of Amminadab, Amminadab the father of Nahshon, and Nahshon the father of Salmon. Salmon was the father of Boaz by Rahab, Boaz was the father of Obed by Ruth, and Obed the father of Jesse. Jesse was the father of David the king.

Rahab was the mother of Boaz, which made her the great, great grandmother of King David, and Jesus Christ comes into the world as the Savior of the world in the lineage of David. How amazing is our God that He takes a lost, hurting, broken, ripped-off little girl that the world would call a prostitute, and reveals Himself to her so that by faith she is delivered from destruction, brought into the community of faith and ultimately ends up in the genealogy of Jesus Christ, and pointed to in Scripture as an exemplar of great faith. How incredible is that? That's what can happen when we trust Him.

11

FAITH
WARRING

David and the Rest

And what more shall I say? For time will fail me if I tell of Gideon, Barak, Samson, Jephthah, of David and Samuel and the prophets, who by faith conquered kingdoms, performed acts of righteousness, obtained promises, shut the mouths of lions, quenched the power of fire, escaped the edge of the sword, from weakness were made strong, became mighty in war, put foreign armies to flight. Women received back their dead by resurrection; and others were tortured, not accepting their release, so that they might obtain a better resurrection; and others experienced mockings and scourgings, yes, also chains and imprisonment. They were stoned, they were sawn in two, they were tempted, they were put to death with the sword; they went about in sheepskins, in goatskins, being destitute, afflicted, ill-treated (men of whom the world was not worthy), wandering in deserts and mountains and caves and holes in the ground. And all these, having gained approval through their faith, did not receive what was promised, because God had provided something better for us, so that apart from us they would not be made perfect.

HEBREWS 11:32-40

AS WE COME TO THE LAST NAMES IN THE HALL OF FAITH IN HEBREWS 11, we see a common element: the language of battle and war. This is the grammar of the life of faith. Both the Old Testament and the New Testament overflow with the imagery of warfare. As we consider the life of battle, we realize that every war has its heroes. David stands as perhaps the most obvious hero when it comes to warring by faith, especially when we think of his encounter with Goliath.

Just think of big old Goliath—big and ugly and nasty. Then look at little tiny David, that cute little guy. They stand, face to face, in the Valley of Elah in Israel, ready to do battle. You can imagine the nation of Israel standing on the hills behind David, saying, "Yeah! Go, David!" Those chumps. Cowering in the background as a little boy goes with faith in the God of Israel and takes on that giant. Take a close look at Goliath, because his face tells the whole story—a rock embedded in his forehead, and his eyes rolling back in his head. It's gruesome and awesome at the same time. David's victory shows what God can do in battle with an ordinary person who has big faith.

David vs. Goliath = You vs. Satan

When it comes to warring by faith, David is the preeminent figure, the most well-known hero in the hall of faith. And his encounter with Goliath was profound, because while this story is true—a literal, historical incident—it is also a metaphor. David's encounter with Goliath paints a picture for us of our battle with Satan. As Christians we know that we are engaged in a battle. We know that Christ is battling with Satan and we are a part of that. Goliath can be thought of as a picture of Satan. He was big, intimidating and a mocker—just like Satan. Goliath stood about 9½ feet tall. His armor weighed more than 200 pounds. The head of his spear weighed 19 pounds.[1]

---

1. See 1 Samuel 17:4-7.

Goliath certainly was one big guy, intimidating to say the least. Satan can be like that in our lives, can't he? Let's be honest. Satan can really mess with us and can seem extremely big, powerful, and intimidating at times. Goliath represents all these characteristics—not only in his physical size, but also in his reputation as a champion of war.

David hadn't been to war. Goliath had. Many of us are new to spiritual warfare. Satan's been doing it for thousands of years. That can be intimidating! Goliath intimidated Israel by shouting every morning and every night for 40 days straight. He was relentless in calling out Israel. Our enemy can be like that. Have you ever felt pursued by Satan, with him just continually, relentlessly attacking you, trying to jack up your life? Most of us have.

Mocking Is His M.O.

Goliath liked to mock as well. When David stood up to him, Goliath said, "Am I a dog, that you come to me with sticks? . . . Come to me and I will give your flesh to the birds of the sky and the beasts of the field."[2] He openly mocked David, trying to belittle and intimidate him. The enemy does that to us. Not only is he a liar, but he is also a mocker. He loves to mock and intimidate us, especially when we're endeavoring to live a life of faith.

The enemy calls out our frailties because he knows we're already self-conscious and insecure about them. David was aware of his weaknesses. He knew his youth and size made him the underdog. Goliath strategically mocked David in an effort to build up his own position and remind David of his low chance of victory. The enemy loves to mock, but we are called to be strong in the strength of the Lord and *His* might—not in any strength of our own.[3] Little David had "God confidence"—another name for faith—as he faced that giant.

---

2. 1 Samuel 17:43-44.
3. See Ephesians 6:10.

So after Goliath spoke, he came right back at the giant with some words of his own. In 1 Samuel 17:26 he said, "Who is this uncircumcised Philistine, that he should taunt the armies of the living God?" As a Jew, it wasn't exactly a compliment to say to someone, "You uncircumcised person, you." That's because circumcision was the sign of the Covenant. It was a sign that you were in relationship with God, that you belonged to God, and that God was on your side. David's carefully chosen words pointed out that Goliath was none of those. I love David's boldness as he calls Goliath out with that one.

In battle, Goliath tried to intimidate David by reminding him of his size. But David turned right back around and reminded Goliath that he didn't belong to the one true God. You can do the same. The next time Satan reminds you of your past, remind him of his future. The Bible says that Satan is going to the lake of fire and that he will be tormented there for eternity.[4] The Bible doesn't teach that hell is a big party and that Satan is the Emcee. That's *not* what the Bible says, in case you were wondering. The Bible says that hell is a place of darkness and weeping and gnashing of teeth.[5] There's a worm that devours the flesh and never dies, and Satan will be tormented in that place.[6] But still he loves to mock us and remind us of our past—even if it was just five minutes ago. So the next time Satan reminds you of your past, you remind him of his future. Your past might be horrible, but his future is worse. Your past is covered under the blood of Jesus, and his future is coming at the hand of Jesus. You remind him of that. You let him know like David did Goliath.

The Source of David's Boldness

David had a simple reason for his boldness: the fight wasn't about him. He knew at that young age that the fight was all about God.

---

4. See Revelation 20:10.
5. See Matthew 8:12; 13:42.
6. See Mark 9:48.

David was convinced of the supremacy of God, the value of God, and the purposes of God. And so for David's life it wasn't about David. That can become routine for us to say; it can become part of our Christianese to say, "It's not about me." But we really need to lay hold of that statement and understand its significance, because we *do* have a tendency to make it about us. It's just human nature. We need a bigger picture of the supremacy of Christ, the glory of Christ and the mission of Christ, and our lives should be subsumed by and submitted to Him. Our lives should be humbled under the mighty hand of God.[7] We just make too much of ourselves, don't we? But David knew better. For him it was all about living for the one true God and His purposes.

Conflict Is a Given

As we look at David and the others in Hebrews 11:32-40, we realize all mission faces opposition. This is of profound importance to understand. If we're on a mission, we're going to encounter opposition. If you make yourself useful in the kingdom of God, you will experience some severe opposition. You will experience battle, or as we call it in the Church, "spiritual warfare." So when we talk about "warring by faith," we need to realize that *warfare is the normal state of the Christian life.* Our normal state is to be at battle with the powers of darkness, with the schemes of Satan. We experience some times of rest and peace, but they are few and far between. Likewise, the Christian life will be one of conflict. As Christians, we will live in a state of warfare most of the time, because the Christian life is a call to mission. That's really the issue. We are called to mission.

Extraordinary or Just Extraordinarily Used?

Now here's the good news about being on mission. I want you to be encouraged by this. *You do not need to be extraordinary to be extraordinarily used.*

---

7. See 1 Peter 5:6.

You really don't. I mean, these guys mentioned here in Hebrews 11:32—Gideon, Barak, Samson, Jephthah, David and Samuel—they weren't necessarily extraordinary in and of themselves.

Think about Gideon. You recall his story from Judges 6-7. Gideon was a frightened farmer. When the Lord came to him, He found Gideon threshing wheat—in a wine vat. You're supposed to thresh wheat on a high mound because you throw the wheat into the air and the wind comes and separates the chaff from the wheat. But Gideon hid down in a wine vat, something built into the ground, trying to sift the wheat. There's no wind down there. Threshing doesn't even work.

Now, we know from the story of Gideon that when God would tell Gideon something, he would say, "Okay, God, but are You sure? Let me put out this fleece, and if You make the fleece wet and the ground dry, I'll know You are serious." God would do exactly what Gideon wanted Him to do. But that wasn't enough for Gideon. He went back and said, "Okay, God, are You sure? Let me put the fleece out again, and this time do the opposite—keep the fleece dry and make the ground wet."[8] That's where we get the expression "putting out a fleece."

God was patient with Gideon—just like He is with us. We put out the fleece all the time, don't we? We say, "Oh, if God wants me to marry that girl, then when she comes and sees me she'll have a Channel Islands surfboard and it'll be pink and I'll know that she's the one for me. That's my fleece before the Lord." It's just that stupid, but we all do it. Don't be afraid to admit it.

Gideon demonstrated a lack of faith, not an exercise of faith. God had already told him what to do! But God was gracious; He met Gideon in his weakness and fear and lack of faith and threw him a bone with that whole fleece thing. And even when God spoke, Gideon didn't grow in faith right away—*yet God used him radically.*

---

8. See Judges 6:36-37.

Barak's Battle

Barak had a simple task: lead Israel in a battle against Sisera, the commander of the Canaanite army. Now, the Canaanite army had 900 iron chariots while Israel didn't have *any* chariots, much less iron chariots. Barak was told by Deborah, the prophetess and judge of Israel at the time, that God had commanded him to go to war against Sisera, and that God would give him the victory. But Barak didn't believe he could do it—even with that assurance! He must have been afraid of those iron chariots and all those Canaanite troops. Barak told Deborah that he needed her to go with him or he wasn't going. Deborah's response is not surprising: "Wow, dude. I'll go with you, but the honor is not going to be yours. It's going to be a woman who gets Sisera—not you."[9] And that's just what happened. Deborah went with him, they won the battle and ultimately another woman, Jael, killed Sisera by driving a tent peg through his head. These were some serious chicks![10]

Like Gideon, Barak was out of place. He should have been warring, but instead he was scared and intimidated. Yet God still used him radically and led him to victory against an enemy a lot bigger and stronger than he. That should be an encouragement to each of us who falter in our faith, who aren't as strong as we would like to be, who aren't as extraordinary as we had imagined ourselves. God uses non-extraordinary people for extraordinary purposes.

Samson and His Ladies

Samson is another great example of God using someone not really worthy in the eyes of most. If you've read about him in Judges 13–16, you know that Samson was not the most godly man. He had a thing for the ladies. He yielded to his fleshly appetites often, and that got him in a lot of trouble. Yet God still used him radically. Samson had

---

9. See Judges 4:9.
10. See Judges 4:1–5:31 for the whole story.

some moments of great faith. He trusted the Lord at a time when it really counted. He was willing to give his life to defeat the enemy at the end. He's remembered for his great physical strength, but when it came to his morals, he was pretty weak.

So Should I Follow Their Example?

Some people read the Bible with a degree of naiveté and say, "Well, look at these guys! They were blowing it and God used them, so maybe I should just blow it and count on God using me." While it's easy to see the thought process, that's the wrong kind of thinking because we're called to holiness and righteousness. So what these stories teach us is *not* that we ought to be like Samson and give in to the fleshly appetites, or be like Barak and Gideon and give in to intimidation. We're not called to be immoral or weak and fearful. It's just the opposite. We are called to be pure, holy, strong, courageous and filled with faith. What these stories *do* teach us is that God is merciful, and that sometimes He blesses us in spite of us. That's a biggie, because we tend to get too religious. We like to think that God blesses us *because of us*. We start saying, "God, thanks for blessing me, but I know that You're really blessing me because, well, I'm me. I mean, why wouldn't You bless me?"

The reality is that God blesses us *in spite of us*, according to who He is, not who we are. He does not bless us *for us*. This is huge! In the Abrahamic Covenant—which is foundational to our understanding of mission—God came to Abraham and said, "I will make you a great nation and nations, and I will bless you and in you all the nations of the earth will be blessed." He blessed Abraham and his descendants *so that they might bless others*. Whenever God blesses us, there is an expectation from Him that we will then, in turn, bless others. He doesn't bless you just for you. You're a part of that equation, but you're not the totality.

However God is blessing you—if it's a spiritual gift that He has given you, if it's financial, if it is a certain ability or talent, if it's influence or anything else—He is blessing you so that you might bless others, so that ultimately He might be adored among all the peoples. That's mission. That's what we're supposed to be involved in. And it's all done for His own glory—in spite of us. He can use each of us radically, for His extraordinary purposes.

God's Promises Are for His Purposes

God made radical promises to Israel. He not only made them a nation, but He also said He would chasten them, and that once He did, He would bring them back to the Promised Land. At the same time, He told them, "I'm not bringing you back to the land for you; I'm doing it for My glory." Ezekiel 36:22 says:

> Therefore say to the house of Israel, "Thus says the Lord GOD, 'It is not for your sake, O house of Israel, that I am about to act, but for My holy name, which you have profaned among the nations where you went.'"

Like Israel, we tend to make it all about us. We make the promises He gives about us and lose the kingdom perspective. But God doesn't do things merely for us. God does things for His glory. If God did things solely for us, He would be corrupt because we are corrupt.

Jephthah

Jephthah is the next person mentioned in the hall of faith in Hebrews 11, and his is another story of someone with a bad past that God used for His good purposes. Judges 11 tells us that Jephthah the Gileadite was a valiant warrior but also the son of a prostitute. He didn't have the best past. His brothers shunned him and he later ran around with the wrong crowd. Over the course of his life, he made some really bad calls. He ended up having to kill his only child, a daughter, and offer her as a sacrifice because of a rash vow that he made. But here he is in the Hall of Faith. God used him radically, because Jephthah was in it for God and not himself.

David Had His Problems, Too

Yes, David was a man after God's own heart. We also know him to be a great warrior and the greatest king of Israel. He was a lion killer, a bear killer and a giant slayer. But let's not forget his adulterous and murderous ways. Knowing that should not make us feel better about our own sin. What it should do is increase our understanding of how merciful and good and powerful God is in our lives. It should help us realize that God can use us in spite of us and bless us in spite of us. After hearing the stories of these flawed people that God used so powerfully, there is no other response than to say, "God is good and kind, and He deserves all the glory." In 1 Corinthians 1:26, Paul says:

> For consider your calling, brethren, that there were not many wise according to the flesh, not many mighty, not many noble; but God has chosen the foolish things of the world to shame the wise, and God has chosen the weak things of the world to shame the things which are strong, and the base things of the world and the despised God has chosen, the things that are not, so that He may nullify the things that are, so that no man may boast before God. But by His doing you are in Christ Jesus, who became to us wisdom from God, and righteousness and sanctification, and redemption, so that, just as it is written, "Let him who boasts, boast in the Lord."

So these stories of weak men with great failures who were nevertheless used greatly by God should not cause us to feel better about our sin or more optimistic about our sinful state. Instead, they should render us more dependent upon God, more in awe of God, more zealous to bring God glory and to see Him use us in spite of us. That fact—

that God chooses to use us in spite of us—should really humble us. And yes, there should come a degree of optimism, but not about our sin. What we should be optimistic about is the character of Christ. If God can use us so powerfully even in our failures and frailties, how much more could He use us if we were pursuing strength and holiness? Strive to be the most effective you can be for the kingdom and the glory of God by trusting more and sinning less.

Faith at the Pivotal Moments

As I mentioned earlier in this book, if we took the totality of the lives of all the men and women found in the Hall of Faith and looked at their entire lives—not just the highlights—they could just as easily be found in the Hall of Shame. They were not necessarily great people in and of themselves. But they had great faith at pivotal moments. They didn't have great faith all the time, but at critical junctures in their lives they exercised great faith in a great God. And as a result, God used them for great deeds.

These people conquered kingdoms, performed acts of righteousness, obtained promises, shut the mouths of lions, quenched the power of fire, and escaped the edge of the sword. From weakness they were made strong, became mighty in war and put foreign armies to flight. There again we see the language of conflict and the imagery of war. They engaged in war because they cared about God's mission. They were sold out for God's purposes.

No Mission Without Opposition

Now if you want to avoid spiritual warfare and conflict, just sit on the sidelines. Just take yourself out of the game. But if you want to be in mission, there's going to be opposition. There is no mission without opposition. Jesus said this in Matthew 16:18: "I will build My church; and the gates of Hades will not overpower it."

That is warfare language. Those are fighting words, filled with conflict and aggression. "I'm building My Church," He's saying. There's forward momentum. He is on the aggress. So while the gates of Hades are defensive and retentive and are there to keep people in, the kingdom of God is liberating and expansive. God is on the offensive, trying to free people from bondage. He's building His church and the gates of hell are trying to defend against it and He is saying that they will not prevail. That's conflict language that clearly speaks of victory. Jesus Christ and His purposes will be victorious, but be prepared for a fight.

I'll tell you how this principle is working out in the life of our church. As I write this, we are in the middle of planting a church in San Francisco. Jesus is building His Church in that city, and we are with Him. He's on the move, doing a good thing, and using us for His purposes. As a result, we are experiencing conflict and opposition. We are being hit with spiritual warfare because we are in the middle of a war.

One way the enemy typically tries to oppose us is by attacking our families. And Satan is such a jerk. I just hate the guy. In fact, he likes to go after our kids. Did you ever notice that? Because I know Satan wants to attack my kids, I walk around the perimeter of my house and I rebuke Satan and his forces. I go to the end of my street and I stand there praying. I rebuke Satan and I pray the covering of Jesus Christ over my street from perverts, from cars driving too fast, and from any other destructive plan of the enemy. I go into my kids' rooms in the middle of the night when they're sleeping, stand with my arms lifted high and I pray over them, verbally rebuking Satan. I lay my hands on them and pray the blessings of God on them. I pray for their hearts, that their little hearts will be given to Jesus and the mission of Christ, and that they will begin, at a young age, to realize the glory of Christ. I pray that they would live with great power for His purposes. I pray that my daughter, little Daisy Love, would be radical for Jesus, and that my son, Isaiah, would be a powerful warrior for Him.

But you can expect backlash when you pray like that. There are physical manifestations of Satan that will come, because no mission is without opposition. When the opposition comes, you've got to fight. Remember that we don't fight in the physical realm; our battle is a spiritual one. As Paul says in 2 Corinthians 10:3-4:

> For though we walk in the flesh, we do not war according to the flesh, for the weapons of our warfare are not of the flesh, but divinely powerful for the destruction of fortresses.

John Piper says, "Life is war because the maintenance of our faith and the laying hold of eternal life is a constant fight. Paul makes it clear in 1 Thessalonians 3:5 that Satan targets our faith for destruction."[11] The kingdom of God is going forward and setting people free, but it's a battle. The battle is fought in your homes, in your marriage, in your church and in your workplace. To win it, we must be men and women who see the value of Christ and His mission and are willing to live in a state of conflict.

Life During Wartime

In his excellent book *Don't Waste Your Life*, Piper talks about the need to live with a "wartime mindset." He describes this idea by saying, "It tells me that there's a war going on in the world between Christ and Satan, truth and falsehood, belief and unbelief. It tells me that there are weapons to be funded and used, but that these weapons are not swords or guns or bombs, but the gospel and prayer and self-sacrificial love. And it tells me that the stakes are higher than any other war in history. They are eternal and infinite. They are heaven and hell, eternal joy or eternal torment (Matthew 25:46)."[12] He goes on to say that we need to remind ourselves that we don't live in peacetime, but as Christians on

---

11. John Piper, "A Battle Call to Advance God's Kingdom," *Mission Frontiers,* March-April, pp. 13-15.
12. John Piper, *Don't Waste Your Life* (Wheaton, IL: Crossway Books, 2007), pp. 111-112.

mission we live in wartime and we need to have a wartime mentality. You see, when a nation goes to war, it affects their financial reality. It affects the way they work.

Part of the city of San Francisco's history is that during World War II, they set aside the search for gold and instead started making iron and building ships for the war effort. The whole city gave itself to that endeavor, and during that time, the city saw an increased desire for family life, righteousness and godliness. It only lasted until the late 1960s, but there was a definite change in behavior that accompanied this wartime mentality.

Today, too many Christians are walking around with a peacetime mentality. There's no thought about the financial reality of us being at war. They're not funding the weapon of the gospel. They're not funding soldiers that are going into battle. They're not giving to the Church that Christ is building to push back the forces of darkness and to crash down the gates of hell. Instead, they're living as if it were peacetime. Their hope and joy is in this world and all they can see is what's before them. Because of this, the Body is hampered and limping—because not all of its parts are functioning and not everyone is participating.

Some of us are sleeping, and it's high time that we awake. "Awake, sleeper, and arise from the dead!" Paul said to the church in Ephesus.[13] He also told the church in Rome that they needed to wake up and realize the times they were living in; that Jesus was coming soon and it was time to stop sinning and get in the game.[14] There's a spiritual battle going on around us for our kids, for our marriages, for our communities, for our churches and for Christ's church as a whole. We're at war. Are you in the battle or are you on the bench? It's one or the other. And if you're in the battle, it's not part-time; it's full-time. It's all the time, because it's wartime.

---

13. Ephesians 5:14.
14. See Romans 13:11-14.

It's normal for the Christian life to be a life of conflict. In 2 Timothy 2:3, Paul said, "Suffer hardship with me, as a good soldier of Christ Jesus." Then in verse 4 he adds this commentary, "No soldier in active service entangles himself in the affairs of everyday life, so that he may please the one who enlisted him as a soldier." In other words, they are fully given to the task. Paul is not suggesting that we shouldn't live our lives. He's just saying that we should *be fully given to the task*. We cannot allow our hope, our joy, our identity, our security and our whole future to be tied up in this world. This world is a rip-off. It will let us down and disappoint us. But Christ is worth living for.

The Consequences of Warfare

When men and women, in the name of Jesus, by the power of the Holy Spirit, go to war, they see and experience real victories. When I stand in my kids' rooms and pray over them, there is victory in Jesus. As you pray for your community, there is victory in your community.

Hebrews 11:33-34 describes the kind of victories that God accomplished through the men and women in the Hall of Faith. They conquered kingdoms, escaped the edge of the sword, became mighty in war, put foreign armies to flight, and a lot more. All those victories were real and tangible and transformative. When we engage in the kingdom of God moving forward, it is transformative for us and our families and our communities. Throughout history God has changed whole cities when His people entered the spiritual battle. At one point, the entire Roman Empire was declared a Christian empire.[15] The whole world can change when the gospel goes forth.

---

15. Admittedly, many may not view this as a positive event in the advance of the Church. Some would say that the Church moved at this juncture from being dynamic and revolutionary to being static and institutionalized. For example, see Michael Frost and Alan Hirsch, *The Shaping of Things to Come* (Peabody, MA: Hendrickson Publishers, 2003), pp. 8-9. This may be correct, but my point here remains that the Church had come a long way in its spread and influence since its birth in Jerusalem.

But there are also consequences on the other side. We are almost guaranteed to see some apparent losses. Hebrews 11:35 starts out by saying that "women received back their dead by resurrection." But then it says, "and others were tortured, not accepting their release, in order that they might obtain a better resurrection," speaking of the ultimate resurrection. The next three verses say that others experienced mocking and scourging, chains and imprisonment. They were stoned, they were sawn in two, they were tempted, they were put to death with swords, they went about in sheepskins and goatskins, being destitute, afflicted, ill-treated. They were men of whom the world was not worthy.

Every war has casualties, and this one is no different. Make no mistake about it. There are victories and there are *apparent* losses. Make sure you notice the word "apparent" there. There are apparent losses. The transition in Hebrews 11:35 is important. It tells us that not *all* men and women of faith experience miraculous deliverance. This is contrary to the health-and-wealth gospel that's so popular in America.

In my Bible, not everybody is delivered. We still have martyrs today. About 176,000 Christians will be killed this year for their belief in Jesus Christ.[16] Many will be tortured beyond what we can speak of. They had real faith. And God honored their faith. It wasn't a faith issue. You can't say, "Oh, if they just had enough faith, it wouldn't have happened to them." That's not what the Bible teaches. Just look at the people in the Hall of Faith. They are given as examples of great faith and yet horrible things happened to many of them.

Faith, Even When He Does Not Deliver Us

Sometimes more faith is required to *endure* hardship than to *escape* hardship. Great faith is needed to continue to trust Jesus Christ in the

---

16. According to the World Evangelical Alliance, more than 200 million Christians in at least 60 countries are denied fundamental human rights solely because of their faith. David B. Barrett, Todd M. Johnson and Peter F. Crossing, in their 2009 report in the *International Bulletin of Missionary Research* (vol. 33, no. 1, p. 32), estimate that approximately 176,000 Christians will have been martyred from mid-2008 to mid-2009.

face of trials and tribulations and tragedy. We need to learn to trust and obey God, even if He doesn't deliver us from our present circumstances. You're not always delivered. Like Shadrach, Meshach and Abednego, we need to be ready to trust God *even if He does not deliver us*. These three guys were asked to worship a statue of the king. They refused, even though they knew King Nebuchadnezzar would throw them into his fiery furnace. They refused because they knew it was the right thing to do, and they had faith that God would see them through. What's even more amazing is that they were ready to face the furnace even if God would not deliver them from the fire. We see this faith expressed in Daniel 3:16-18:

> O Nebuchadnezzar, we do not need to give you an answer concerning this matter. If it be so, our God whom we serve is able to deliver us from the furnace of blazing fire; and He will deliver us out of your hand, O king. But even if He does not, let it be known to you, O king, that we are not going to serve your gods or worship the golden image that you have set up.

Shadrach, Meshach and Abednego were committed to God's purposes and to God's glory no matter what. They believed God would deliver them. They believed it, but they also said, "Even if He doesn't, we're trusting Him absolutely." God delivered them from the fire, without even a hair singed or the scent of smoke on their clothes![17] It is faith like that—even when it *does* result in martyrdom and suffering—that brings glory to God.

The Glory in Suffering

In the life of faith, we experience victories and apparent losses. Both can bring glory to God. If God was not glorified in the deaths of these

---

17. Check out the full story (it's a good one) in Daniel 3.

martyrs, they wouldn't be mentioned in the Hall of Faith. You see, often our perspective is wrong. We think to ourselves, *If everything came out great, then I must have had the right faith. I must have made the right moves.* But step back for a moment and think about it. Millions of Christians throughout history made the right moves and were tortured or executed for their faith. As I mentioned earlier, it's still happening today

A paradox in Christian history and theology goes something like this: *There is glory in suffering, because in our suffering, Jesus Christ is glorified.* The apostles realized this. After being flogged for preaching and teaching Jesus, we see them in Acts 5:41-42 rejoicing:

> So they went on their way from the presence of the Council, rejoicing that they had been considered worthy to suffer shame for His name. And every day, in the temple and from house to house, they kept right on teaching and preaching Jesus as the Christ.

Somehow in their shame glory came to the name of Jesus Christ. Suffering is not merely the *result* of glorifying Jesus and being on mission, but it is also the *means* of glorifying Jesus and being on mission. First Peter 4:13,16 says:

> But to the degree that you share the sufferings of Christ, keep on rejoicing, so that also at the revelation of His glory you may rejoice with exultation . . . but if anyone suffers as a Christian, he is not to be ashamed, but is to glorify God in this name.

A Miracle Happens

Suffering and martyrdom glorify Jesus Christ when a faithful witness for the Lord shares the truth in love and meets suffering or death with joy. The eyes of unbelievers are opened when that happens. That's exactly what happened to the Roman centurion at the cross of Jesus Christ. When he saw how Jesus died, he said, "Truly this man was the Son of

God!"[18] There was something in the righteous death of Jesus that opened this man's eyes, removed the blinders and caused him to see that this really was the Son of God.

And when men and women today give themselves to suffering, persecution and martyrdom, the scales fall off of eyes and people see the truth. History tells us that the Church grows fastest where the persecution is worst. That's why Tertullian, a Christian apologist and author, wrote in A.D. 197, "The blood of the martyrs is the seed of the Church."[19] History has proven that where the opposition is greatest, where men and women are giving up their lives, many lives will also be saved. Christians were dying in the Roman coliseums, being thrown to the lions, being made sport of because of their faith. But the Roman people saw that those Christians didn't fear death, and by the fourth century that whole nation was declared a Christian nation.

Martyrdom glorifies Jesus Christ because it is proof of a purpose in this world that's bigger than the individual.[20] It's proof that Jesus Christ conquered death through the cross and the resurrection. It shows the world that the sting of death has been removed. In 1 Corinthians 15:55, Paul says, "O, death, where is your victory? O death, where is your sting?" The fear of death is gone.

God allows people to be martyred. I don't know how to say it other than that. There is simply no way to soften the message. But don't forget that when they die, they go to glory and achieve the fulfillment of their life's goal: to glorify Christ. It's just like Paul said in Philippians 1:19-21:

> I know that this will turn out for my deliverance through your
> prayers and the provision of the Spirit of Jesus Christ, according

---

18. Mark 15:39.
19. Quintus Septimius Florens Tertullianus (c. A.D. 160–220), *Apologeticus*, chapter 50.
20. Don't confuse the validity of Christian martyrdom with the martyrdom we see in Islam. In Islam the goal of the martyrs is to kill other people in the process of killing themselves. In Christianity we are talking about Christians being killed by people who are not being threatened in any physical way. Big difference!

to my earnest expectation and hope, that I will not be put to shame in anything, but that with all boldness, Christ will even now, as always, be exalted in my body, whether by life or by death. For to me, to live is Christ and to die is gain.

Living for Him

The good news is that most of us haven't been called to die for Christ—at least not yet! Instead, we've been called to live for Him. The call you need to answer is the one to live for Christ and His mission. And remember, living on mission means there's going to be opposition. As Paul says in 2 Corinthians 4:16-18:

> Therefore we do not lose heart, but though our outer man is decaying, yet our inner man is being renewed day by day. For momentary, light affliction is producing for us an eternal weight of glory far beyond all comparison, while we look not at the things which are seen, but at the things which are not seen; for the things which are seen are temporal, but the things which are not seen are eternal.

Get your eyes off this world and the things of this world. There is a far weightier glory in eternity than in this life. The life of faith is filled with warfare and opposition, but ultimately Jesus Christ wins. For our lives today, His grace is more than enough. Jesus didn't pull any punches. He said, "You want to follow Me? You've got to count the cost." So while He may never call you to die for Him, He is calling you right now to live for Him.

Remember Who Wins

As we close this chapter, think of the giants you're facing in your life right now—and then remember little David taking down Goliath.

Where is the enemy trying to take ground in your family? Where is he trying to keep people captive? It's time to go to war, brothers and sisters. Learn to do battle in the spiritual realm. Study Ephesians 6 and pay heed to James 4. Prepare for war and get ready for victory because the gates of hell will not prevail against the going forth of the Church. Don't miss out. Don't sit on the bench. Identify what God is doing in your marriage, in your family, in your community, in this nation and in this generation, and get on mission. Get on board. Get in the battle. Because whether you live or die, Jesus wins. He is Christ our Victor, and He is worthy of our faith.

EPILOGUE

We all want to be known as people of faith—people who live our lives the way God wants us to. But many of us feel disqualified already. Many of you think that you're just too far gone for God to use you. If that's you, you need to read your Bible!

Look at the stories of the heroes of this faith. Rahab was a prostitute, Noah was a drunk, Abraham was way too old, Isaac was a daydreamer, Jacob was a liar, Leah was ugly, Joseph was abused, Moses couldn't speak well, Gideon was afraid, Samson had long hair and was a womanizer, Jeremiah and Timothy were too young, David had an affair and was a murderer, Elijah was suicidal, Isaiah preached naked, Jonah ran from God, Naomi was a widow, Job went bankrupt, John the Baptist ate bugs, Peter denied Jesus, the disciples fell asleep while praying, Martha worried about everything, Mary Magdalene was demon possessed, the Samaritan woman was divorced many times, Zacchaeus was too small, Paul was too religious, Timothy had an ulcer, and Lazarus was dead!

When you look at that list, you really have no excuses. These are the examples given to us in God's Word. They weren't great people, but they had great moments of faith in a great God. At the critical moments of their lives, they exercised great faith and made the right faith decisions. We can do the same. We can lead lives that are pleasing to God, not because we are great people, but because by faith we can connect with a great God. When we place our faith in the one true God, we can accomplish great things for His glory.

As William Carey, missionary to India and the father of modern missions, once said, "Expect great things from God. Attempt great things for God." When you do, great things will happen—because our God is great. Choose to live by faith in Him, and watch what happens. That's when things start getting good.

ABOUT THE AUTHOR

Britt Merrick grew up near Santa Barbara, California, in a little beach town called Carpinteria. In his childhood years Britt's singular passion was surfing, and soon he was making surfboards for some of the best surfers in the world alongside his father, Al Merrick, at the Channel Islands, Inc. surfboard factory—the largest and probably most famous surfboard company in the world. Britt was also handling the company's advertising, marketing, and amateur surf team. Shortly after re-committing his life to the Lord in his early twenties, Britt began to teach Bible studies at his parents' home for the surfer kids in Carpinteria. These Bible studies eventually led to Britt teaching and preaching at a Friday night college ministry at a church in Santa Barbara. In the fall of 2003, sensing a further call to ministry, Britt, his wife and some close friends started a church called Reality in his hometown of Carpinteria. Reality Carpinteria is active in and passionate about youth, community transformation, birthing new churches, sending missionaries overseas, and equipping the next generation of leaders. By the grace and to the glory of God, the Reality network of churches has grown to include churches in Los Angeles and Stockton, California, and soon London and San Francisco. Britt continues to pastor full-time. He loves his wife, Kate, their son, Isaiah, and daughter, Daisy Love, the Bible and, of course, Jesus and His Church.

For more information about Britt Merrick, visit
www.brittmerrick.com

Never Before Published Titles from
A.W. Tozer

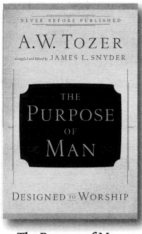

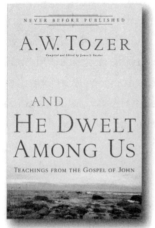